small fires

SMALL FIRES

essays

Julie Marie Wade

Sarabande  Books

LOUISVILLE, KENTUCKY

Managing Editor
Sarabande Books, Inc.
2234 Dundee Road, Suite 200
Louisville, KY 40205

Library of Congress Cataloging-in-Publication Data

Wade, Julie Marie.
Small fires / by Julie Marie Wade.
    p. cm.
Essays.
ISBN 978-1-936747-02-3 (pbk. : alk. paper)
I. Title.
PS3623.A345S63 2011
814'.6—dc22
[B]
                                    2011007020

Cover and text design by Kirkby Gann Tittle.
Manufactured in Canada.
This book is printed on acid-free paper.

Sarabande Books is a nonprofit literary organization.

The Kentucky Arts Council, the state arts agency, supports Sarabande Books with state tax dollars and federal funding from the National Endowment for the Arts.

For Angie
Amor Vincit Omnia

Here, houselights blink on,
the breeze empties
of warmth. And more often
I catch myself

in these moments
when the light is scarcely
alive above the roofs
and I lean on the doorframe,
remembering the small

fires of everything gone.
I no longer know who
I'm waiting for. I ask
everything of the stillness.
I wait for everyone.

—Rick Barot, from "Blue Hours" [II. The Exile]

Contents

SMALL FIRES

Keepsake

I ask my grandmother what she will contribute to our time capsule. The year is 1989, and Joy, Alicia, and I have resolved to commemorate the passing of our first decade. After many long hours scouting the neighborhood, we have even agreed on a place—Pine Cone Island—a plot of land perfectly centralized, walking distance from our respective houses, wild and grassy where neighbor boys play ball, but with a cozy corner inlet of hunkering pines and soft soil ideal for digging.

Grandma June has been around a long time. She was born in 1911, which means she has nearly reached her eighth decade. Fauntlee Hills, where she has lived since 1953, is a beautiful, tiered community built on bluffs overlooking Puget Sound. The uniform brick houses, with their varying views of the sea, are primarily occupied by first-generation residents. Not first generation in the U.S. per se—though my grandmother is, eighth child of Swedish immigrant parents—but first generation in this historic neighborhood, its 1950s cocoon of widowed women whose children have grown up to leave them, whose husbands have long since passed away.

"Do women always live longer than men?" I ask.

"Not always, but often," she replies. Grandma is wrapped in her shawl, blouse-sleeves tucked with tissues and a crossword puzzle in hand.

"Why is that, Grandma?"—thinking of Mrs. Niemi, who is still Mrs. Niemi, even though her husband disappeared into death three years ago. And Mrs. Rothman, and Mrs. Kaufman, and Mrs. Berg.

"I don't rightly know," comes her patient reply. "Maybe we're just less willing to go."

I wonder why my grandfather went and what he would have put in my capsule. "Probably a hymn book," she tells me, "because your grandpa loved to sing so much. He was a tenor in the Phinney Ridge Lutheran Church choir."

"But what about *you*?" I sit beside her at the ancient oak table, legs swinging but because I am tall, my tennis shoes scrape on the floor.

"Well, that's a hard question," my grandmother says. "What I love best I like to keep with me."

Recently, at my school's roller-skating party, I have commenced a secret romance. The boy I think I love, whose mother wears glossy lip paint and a cream sweater with creased peach pants and matching starched peach collar, does not attend; his family ice-skates on Saturdays, and Erich has no intention of trading his blades for wheels. I don't know Lee Bennett's mother since he walks to school with only his older brother. They are both big for their age, tall and filled out across the chest and shoulders, Lee sporting his first dark whiskers along his cheeks and chin, Ryan buying cigarettes easily at thirteen. But when I think of Erich, I see his mother clearly. She is blond and fair-complected, a teacup of a woman with dainty features and a pleasant, docile wave. I want him to invite me over to play Jenga and Pictionary, but mostly so we can eat cheese sandwiches on white triangles of bread, which I am certain his mother takes great care to cut the crusts from, placing a crisp pickle alongside and pouring a cold glass of milk from a brand-name bottle.

"What's your mother's name?" I ask Lee as we lace fingers for our first-ever couples skate. The lights are dimming now; strobes of red and blue cast dizzy shapes across the floor.

"Rosemary," he says. "Why?"

I adore her name at once, conjuring the image of a stone cottage in the woods with a chimney stolidly puffing. Ivy winds around the curtain-clad windows, and this herb called *rosemary*, which I have never seen, blooms in tiny baskets on each ledge.

"No reason"—though I think I can love him now, having determined that he comes from good people.

Lee and I begin to see more of each other. At recess, we walk the playground's perimeter, hand in hand, and I take a certain pleasure in the jealousy our love provokes in others. Sometimes I can hardly hear what he is saying as I watch the swiveling of heads, the shifting hips of bodies, the girls who call me "freak" and "four eyes" suddenly covetous of what I have. This must be commemorated. I am not so naïve as to believe that Lee and I can last forever, but the memory of us must somehow be preserved.

On little squares of steno paper, I write him love notes. *You are more exquisite than a common loon. I long for you like a mustard seed for rain.* Drawing from our class project on John James Audubon and parables turned rote in Bible school, I craft my images, draft my devotion to the boy whose mysterious mother has come to haunt my dreams.

He reciprocates: *My desk is infested with your poems, and I love them! Your head is as big and round as the sun, your eyes like x-ray vision into my heart.*

I smuggle Lee's letters home inside my parka's zip-out lining. My mother must never discover them, which means late at night I bury these scraps under the Raggedy Ann ceramic planter that sits, replete with artificial flowers, on my windowsill. Evidence accumulates; I will need a shoe box soon.

In the afternoons on Vashon View Street, Joy and I sit outside ogling the islands. I ask how her time capsule collection is coming along, and she beams with pride. Her toy box is nearly full.

"But how are we going to bury something that big?"

"I'll have to be selective," she sighs.

After a while, we climb down from the deck and scurry to her backyard's edge, where blackberry bushes thicken and rise and even the bravest dogs won't venture. "It's weatherproof," she says, pointing to the sticker as she pops off the green and yellow plastic lid. "Camouflaged, too."

Inside we find a miracle of things.

"Where did you get these?" I exclaim, incredulous, the forbidden glee of close to forty liquor bottles, piled in careful crosshatch and clinking softly.

"Well, you know Erna Hunt who lives next door?"

I shake my head. "Not really."

"My father always calls her an old drunk, and it's true. When she's been drinking, she comes outside in her bathrobe and screams at her husband in German." Joy leans in close for the juicy gossip, and quoting her mother, recites—"He's kind of a shit you know, what with the other women and all." Then, with a flash of her clear blue eyes: "I figured her trash would tell an interesting tale."

Together Joy and I catalogue the beers and wines in our time capsule ledger, then more attentively the ominously clear bottles. Mrs. Hunt, we notice, seems to have a particular penchant for someone called Mr. Jim Beam.

"And she says her *husband's* the one being unfaithful," Joy smirks. Feeling grown-up and very hush-hush, we do our best to nod and not to laugh.

I realize early on that I have a problem with sharing. Not any essential thing, like food from my lunchbox or toiletries at camp, and anyone who wants can take a sip from my straw. But books I don't like sharing, so I don't understand the library with its Q-cards and barcodes and days when things are due. I resent them, the way I resent the curly-haired librarian with the tight mouth who chides me for talking too loud.

I love books the way some children love stuffed animals, but while they are loving the fur off those plush bodies, the eyes off those velveteen sockets, my books must wear jackets even indoors, and cards tucked in their pockets remind me of their borrowed status, the long tether that trails behind them.

Once, when I was small, we borrowed a puzzle in a plastic bag with white handles that snapped, in a satisfying way, together. My father helped me assemble on the living room floor a spectacular, nearly circus-sized giraffe. But when the time came to take apart the pieces, I kept one. I slipped the giraffe's long neck down the front of my pants and later dislodged it in the bathroom. I couldn't explain, but I didn't think anyone would miss it. That was my token, proof we had completed the puzzle, and more—proof the giraffe had existed at all.

Then, the librarian called: someone had discovered the giraffe had no neck, only a head and the lower half of his torso. "I know you have it, Julie," my father said. "I'll give you till ten to put it back."

He counted, as if we were playing hide-and-go-seek, and when he opened his eyes, there on the rug beside him was the speckled neck, its wood-carved majesty and saffron shading. I, by contrast, was nowhere to be found.

After school, I walked with stealthy determination to Section 600 of the Dewey Decimal System. Here, behind the decorative ferns on the least accessible shelf, I had hidden a book about bodies—an amazing Technicolor accomplishment with provocative illustrations and minimal patches of print. Crouching in a corner chair, legs folded underneath myself, I read greedily, gratuitously, of menstrual cramps and nocturnal emissions. I scoured the written landscape for *sex* and *sexual*, though I disliked equally the sound of *penis* and *vagina*.

When my mother came to find me, I feigned attention to

my work, a ditto of fraction problems spread carefully across my lap.

"Do you need any help with that?" she asked, and I shook my head no, but if she didn't mind, I'd like to stay and finish. Libraries help me clear my head. I concentrate best in such a peaceful environment.

Out of sight again, I slid back the papers like a secret door and gazed again at the bodies. How alive the images were, despite their palpable lack of eroticism. How significant the language was, despite the un-poetics of "training bras" and "pubertal transitions." One day, emboldened by my quickening pulse, my need to know everything and never forget, I slipped the book deep in my schoolbag, inhaled, and sped through the door.

Our friend Alicia lives on the highest tier of the Hills. Her parents are the wealthy Californians my parents grumble about, "poaching all the good land." Joy and I hike dutifully up the long paved path, then turn onto gravel and amble the length of the house.

Alicia's room is admirably private; we can climb in the window without her parents hearing a sound, but then again, they are distracted. Alicia's older brother Tony is brilliant, but the way she explains: "He has trouble dealing with the people side of things." They had to put him in special school and eventually allow him to work at home. When I've seen him, he is pacing the halls, muttering equations and fluttering his hands; sometimes, though faintly, we can hear him humping his mattress in the room next door, which always embarrasses Alicia.

Now there is Norah, the new baby sister her parents didn't expect and of whom they are exceedingly protective. In order to hold her, I have to wash my hands twice with anti-bacterial soap and with Mrs. Feichtmeir always supervising. Her first name is Margo, short for Marguerite, and she is the uppity kind of pretty that makes my teeth chatter and my eyes dart quickly away.

"Spill it," Joy says. "We want to see your provisions."

Alicia kneels down and withdraws from the bottom drawer of her bureau, concealed beneath tidy piles of leotards and tights, a king-sized Hershey bar—"because they might not have them in the future, and chocolate never goes bad, and think how good it would taste if you hadn't had one in fifty years!"—a *Facts of Life* t-shirt she has long since outgrown but doesn't want Norah to inherit; and finally, an assortment of colorful, individually-wrapped candies.

"I've never seen these before," I say, inspecting.

"You haven't?" Joy's eyes grow wide. "My parents' bedside table is full of them."

"Mine too," Alicia nods. "And it's because they ran out that we ended up with my little sister."

In junior confirmation class, we are learning about relics. Many false relics were pawned during the Middle Ages, but I want to know what makes a relic true. "Does it have something to do with faith—how much you believe in the relic?"

Pastor John, whom my parents dislike because he never sports a tie and sometimes wears dock shoes while delivering his sermons, explains that in this instance, faith has nothing to do with it. Some objects are holy, some are profane; some relics are real, others counterfeit. But how could anyone possibly begin to decipher the difference? After all, we are not talking about play money here, where the distinction between George Washington's head and Elmo's or Big Bird's is obvious and passes without comment. Yet, if a society wanted to, it could certainly invalidate the wigged profile of our Founding Father and decide to authenticate—a word I love, as in *true relics required authentication by the Church*—the portrait of Elmo or Big Bird instead.

I resolve to illustrate this contradiction by placing both a Federal Reserve one-dollar bill and a Sesame Street one-dollar note in the time capsule. Fifty years in the future, I reason, they may be equally obsolete.

Meanwhile, I remain unsatisfied regarding the matter of faith. How will I know when I am ready to receive my first communion? How can successful memorization of Luther's *Catechism* constitute preparation for my new responsibilities as a "member of the church"? For one thing, I don't understand why faith seems incompatible with questions, or even, to a greater extent, with doubt. I hear voices on television chime, "Don't take *my* word for it," and I wonder precisely *whose* word we are supposed to take. God's? Our parents'? A school teacher's or trusted friend's? What happens when *their* words start to contradict each other?

My mother kneels at the altar in church, about to consume Christ's metaphorical body and blood. The altar, I infer from its name, is a place where people go to be changed. Until my confirmation, however, I am forced to stay the same, idling like a cold car in winter: to bow my head and receive what has become by now a predictable blessing. This particular Sunday, as I stand in line with my father behind me, I become fixated on the sole of my mother's shoe. There in front of the church, compellingly unaware, she reveals her secret to the entire congregation: the hot pink thrift store sticker with 99¢ printed in bold Magic Marker at its center. Only a minor embarrassment except—my mother has been boasting to the Quilting Club how she does all her shopping at Nordstrom's.

I realize then that I am more interested in lies than truth; that what compels me most is the *maybe* and not the *hard-and-fast*; that I am a disciple of the *possible* and the *what if?* and the *unlikely*. Knowing this, knowing that I make a lousy liar but aspire to be better at it, I am hardly worthy to receive the sacrament of Holy Communion. Can I bow out gracefully? Can I take an extension on my own authentication? What about a "raincheck," like the kind my mother receives in the mail, announcing with stamp and script when the time has come to claim her Kmart treasures?

Instead, on Confirmation Day, I pocket the wafer, swallowing only the wine. I am half-blessed now, half exactly who

I am supposed to be. And in a small envelope in the middle of Revelation, I keep my untouched morsel of holiness, what I will come to think of as my parachute, my *last-chance-dance*, my *just-in-case*.

Most days after school, we stop at my grandmother's house. If I am with my mother, we drink tea and clip coupons. If I am with my father, we eat oatmeal cookies, and I watch as he and my grandma play cribbage. My dad and his mother love coffee. While my own mother protests this beverage that stains teeth and stunts growth and accelerates heart rate and frays nerves, I long for my own white cup and chipped saucer. I long for my place at this table.

The best days are when my aunt has come for a visit. She is single and childless and loves me more than she can say. I reassure her somehow—she who is fraught with terror of female failings, whose face is an open invitation to regret. Since she is often doing laundry, I follow Aunt Linda down into the basement, that labyrinth of leftovers and antique machinery and portals to a distant past.

There is my grandfather's office and his adding machine, everything exactly as he left it: a desk-top calendar from 1971 and the slow-spinning rotary phone where I have recently been caught making prank calls to certain less-than-pleasant neighbors. Beyond this room is my father's college sleep-space, with its thin twin mattress and nautical quilt, its faint odors of Colgate and aftershave. But the room I like best is the old family room, from the days before I was born—when the house was alive with voices and my grandmother could easily descend the stairs.

I ask my aunt again about her bongo drums and the autographed coconut whose signature spells a name I've never heard of. Dutifully, she relays the tale of her graduation travels to Hawaii, her first luau, and the authentic grass skirt she still keeps in her closet. The closet itself is homage to another time.

"One day I'm going to get back into all those clothes

again," she says—"just you wait. I was born a size six, and I intend to die that way."

It doesn't matter that it doesn't make sense, that you're not even a 6X until you turn two or three. I get her meaning. So I don't say what I'm thinking: that she would look silly now, a forty-five-year-old woman dressed in bell bottoms and fur-trimmed boots, prancing around in gold satin shoes and mod space-age dresses. Aunt Linda seems to be searching for her misplaced self in all the most unfulfilling places. She eats and she doesn't get full, but then she gets sick to her stomach. She dyes her hair and complains about the streaking, yet she is paralyzed by the thought of showing gray.

As my aunt, I want her to tell me things my mother never will, to pull back the pages of her cherished *Black Beauty* and reveal a dried and pressed gardenia corsage. I want illicit lovers and torrid affairs with married men, confided only once to a diary called Midge, then locked with a golden key away. At the very least, I want her to tell me about my period, which I am expecting any day now, even though it will be another three years. Girls are maturing faster these days, I read in a book, and surely Aunt Linda could help to pave the way—illuminate the virtues of tampons versus napkins, confirm or disconfirm the rumor that using tampons breaks you the same as your first sex will.

But Aunt Linda is a self-professed "woman of God," a proud, if melancholy, virgin. If she were Catholic, I'm certain she would be a nun. Though in her prime she was too high fashion for habits, there's a kind of saving face involved in celibacy where being "married to God" is concerned. I know because I've thought about it myself: all expenses paid; freedom from expectations concerning men and sex and bodies; lots of time on your own to read and write and pray, which I've decided is reasonably akin to contemplation. But there's also the claustrophobia of the cloister and covering your head and needing to be good all the time and never knowing for sure if you've succeeded.

"Can I have something of yours—to put in my time cap-sule?" I ask, and she gives me a photograph that is dark gray but white around the edges and marked on the back in ballpoint pen: *Linda and Lori, aged 16, fashion models.*

Linda inhabits her body then, the future not yet a foregone conclusion, her fair hair and slender waist and legs that stretch on and on. Lori will face breast cancer and live; Linda will face breast cancer and die. We couldn't know this then, lifting warm clothes from the dryer, listening as the cribbage game unfolds above. We couldn't know this anymore than the young woman in the pho-tograph could know there would come a day when this picture would be all she had left of her story, her self-made myth—that the day would come when she would give even this away.

Lee Bennett and I have been going steady for six months now, which in fourth-grade terms means we have held hands and hugged, but there is pressure to deliver the first kiss, or at least to consent to it. I am not sure which is my responsibility, but I know that I have been withholding.

While I am skeptical about religion and only demi-confirmed, the concept of purity confuses me like decimals. My father says "our bodies are only on loan from God," and my mother says "a girl with a tarnished reputation is on the fast track to becoming a whore." As if that weren't bad enough, I remain uncertain as to whether or not I actually *want* to kiss Lee Bennett. I have been to his house now and baked cookies with his mother, but proximity is no substitute for passion. Once we played Twister, and he fell over on me, and our mouths were very close to touching; even though I was curious, some reflex turned my head away so that he only grazed my cheek. There was awkward silence after. *What was the matter with me?*

I tell Joy and Alicia that I wish I could put my whole self in the time capsule. "Wouldn't it be amazing if we could do it, fast-forward ourselves into the future?"

"But would we get older?" Joy asks.

"And how would we learn anything new?" Alicia wants to know.

"The *world* would be different," I say. "*We* wouldn't have to be."

Joy thinks about it and replies with characteristic alternative-school airs: "I think you're overestimating the relationship between progress and time."

"Not to mention," Alicia interjects, "that even for a short time, burying ourselves alive would be stupid. Didn't you see on *Punky Brewster* when Cherie hid in the old refrigerator? She used up all the oxygen and almost died."

"I saw it," I sigh. "I know it isn't practical. I just wish our time capsule could transform into a time *machine*."

I have continued accumulating artifacts steadily: my best Nerf Turbo football, hot sauce packets from the Taco Bell where my father takes me every Saturday for lunch. Is it my imagination, or is this relationship becoming strained as well?

Things seem fine until we walk down to the park to toss the ball around or wander along the slippery rocks at the shore. My dad says I don't confide in him anymore—not like I used to—and I think it might have something to do with Lee Bennett and needing to make cubbies for parts of my life where there were never compartments before. My thought processes of late have begun to take the shape of waffles: individual squares, thin but significant divisions, each piece pre-apportioned and separate from the rest. For instance, when I think of Lee and imagine kissing him, I cannot, in the same mental space, think of walking through the park with my father. I cannot think of my father at all. And recently, I have learned another meaning of the word *waffle*, which is not just a kind of breakfast food, but also a kind of verb. To waffle means to switch back and forth between possibilities. Some days I feel pretty enough and others like a hideous troll. Sometimes I chatter on and on to God, while others I can't even muster a word, can't even conceive of a Divine Being or a Master Plan.

Despite this waffling, there are a few thoughts I can't pry my mind away from, no matter how hard I try. One of these is Mrs. Miller, who used to be Miss Baer. She tells us the first day of class that her real name is Jani, and her husband's name is Lowell. I don't know why, but I dislike this Lowell already. When she leaves work, Mrs. Miller drives home to Tukwila, a distant suburb, and makes dinner for this man called Lowell. After dinner, she puts on a sweater and walks her dog around the cul-de-sac with this man called Lowell. I look her up in the phone book and find her name second to his: *Lowell and Jani Miller.* I think about sending Lowell an anonymous letter that his wife does not really love him. *But why wouldn't she love him?* my reasonable self inquires. *Why am I so preoccupied?* Then, my other self, the one I favor: *But how could she possibly love a man called Lowell?*

It goes on like this in my mind for months so that I find I am thinking of Mrs. Miller when I am looking for sand crabs with my father or learning to skip stones across still water or drying dishes or practicing my spelling words. And when I finally do kiss Lee Bennett under the mistletoe in fifth grade in my parents' dimly lit hallway, I am *still* thinking of Mrs. Miller and in the dark, I half-despise Lee also, who seems more like a Lowell now, trying to pry apart my lips with his eager tongue.

I fear my mother is jealous that I have not asked her for a token, some piece of memorabilia from her fragile and furious life.

To tell the truth, I am afraid to talk to my mother. She has the uncanny ability to read in my face all that I want not to say. I feel some inexplicable shame for kissing Lee Bennett and allowing him to place his hands where my someday-breasts will be. Too many pillow fights on his mother's bed, and always that sense of myself as a creature capable of being broken. *Why don't boys break?* I wonder. *Why is it only girls?*

In addition, I have started staying after class to clap erasers and wipe down chalkboards for Mrs. Kolbe. She is not warm and tender like Mrs. Miller, whom I secretly call at home and hang up on—just to hear her voice, just to imagine her more clearly in her kitchen, wearing a lavender apron and stirring together hot macaroni with melting cheese. Mrs. Kolbe is a more austere beauty, and her real name is Jennifer, never Jenny, and I am fascinated by her, more even than by any friend's mother. *My* mother must never know about my strange flirtations with authority figures. She would take it personally. She would ask me what these other women could give me that I wasn't getting at home. And I wouldn't be able to answer: not honestly, perhaps not even at all. I would retreat to the safety of the waffle, remind her of my good grades, my made bed.

I love my mother best when she is gardening or decorating. Today she cuts camellias from the tree outside my window, draws a cool bath, and prepares to float these flowers on the surface. She lights candles also, white and pink votives shaped like flowers with smooth undersides for gliding on the water. Guests at her party will come to use the bathroom and be impressed by her perfect orchestration.

"Mom, would you like to give me something for my time capsule—you know, the one Joy and Alicia and I are making?"

She studies me a moment before striking a match and kneeling at the lip of the tub. "No."

"But I thought you would want to, since you like to collect things and put them in curio cabinets." We have eighteen such cabinets now and counting.

"Why would I want my valuables rotting away in the ground? In fifty years, I won't even be around to see them."

It hasn't occurred to me that my mother will die before I will, that this is the most likely course of events. I am sobered by this thought and wonder whether the time capsule itself might be a bad idea. In fifty years, will any of us even care about souvenirs? In fifty years, who will be here to reveal and reclaim them?

I realize, as my mother primps before the bathroom mirror, as she tucks her curled hair behind her ornamented ears, that we are different kinds of collectors. My mother enjoys display, showing off her slew of trinkets, her wall of painted spoons, her shelves and shelves of Precious Moments figurines. There are the vintage phonograph, the hundred records standing in a row, the polished canisters containing ancient sheets of music.

My collection, by contrast, is exclusive contraband: the "Sex" page I tore from the school encyclopedia; the tampon from the broken dispenser at dance; the perfect uncracked sand dollar, with its hidden wealth of white doves and sedimentary stencils; love letters, sent and unsent; a snapshot of Mrs. Miller, swiped from a bulletin board.

"What's your greatest treasure?" I ask my mother.

"You," she replies, without looking up.

"No, I mean—not people, *things*."

"Come here," she says. "Let me show you." I climb up on her bed and watch her sifting through drawers.

She hands me a pair of white baby boots. "These were yours. I'm going to have them bronzed and put them in a glass case on the mantel." Next, she unfolds my birth certificate and a piece of paper with my tiny hand and foot prints. "These I'm going to have framed and hung over the bureau."

Finally, she opens a little wooden chest with enticing red velvet lining. "These are all the teeth you've ever lost," she declares, on a note of pride and poignancy. I have already discovered the tooth fairy is a fraud, but I never imagined my mother hoarding my teeth like the brittle bones of saints, pearly relics of a time gone by.

"Can I have them back?" I want to know.

"*May* I," she corrects—"and no, you may not. They're mine now."

"Well, they came from *my* mouth," I say. "And I'd like to put them in my time capsule."

My mother snatches the chest from my rosy palms and places it back in the drawer. "When you're a mother," she instructs, "you'll understand. You have children, and they start to grow up, but they're still yours, and you don't ever want to lose them."

"But keeping my lost teeth in a box doesn't have much to do with me," I protest.

"Don't be difficult. It has *everything* to do with you. And someday you'll thank me for preserving what you would have otherwise thrown casually away."

I think of her hard hand clutching my wrist as we cross the street, of her teary whispered refrain—"I'd just *die* if anything ever *happened* to you." And I think then I would like to be broken, the way a bottle is sometimes "smashed to smithereens." I could be a smithereen. I could do that job. I could be white foam cresting the waves, like the Little Mermaid after she loses her love. I could be shaken like a soda can until I explode, improper as a double negative or a dandelion in a freshly mowed lawn. Suddenly, it all seems very clear to me: how I don't want to be kept, don't want to be tethered: how, like a human cannonball or a hot air balloon, I belong to the circus—ascension and motion, traveling light, my own life I will have to let go of.

Triptych of My Grandmother:
A Still Life with Three Fruits

First Panel

She comes to this world late—eighth of nine children—fated
to outlive them all. Her husband also. And her youngest child,
the daughter she dotes on for fifty-eight years. *What is the secret
of her stillness?* they wonder. What special interstice does she
inhabit, what footbridge does she tread—resilience to one side,
resignation the other?

She arrives, child of Swedish immigrants, last daughter in
the modest mining town, sent down across the border from
British Columbia into Washington State, the long train ride to
her new high school on Seattle's Capitol Hill. Broadway High.
There in the heart of the city, where the action is, traffic pumps
like oxygen through concrete and cobblestone veins.

On the train, alone for the first time, she studies the silence.
Everywhere these strangers, ensconced in their own lives, and
the fat man in the red coat, eating bananas and staring. His
presence fills her with unspeakable dread, his gaze unlacing
her boots, unfolding her scarf, attempting to dissect her alive.
She moves to a new seat. She clasps her suitcase—blue, with
a hard shell, a polka-dot ribbon tied to the grip, and inside,

those wondrous satin pockets holding her stockings and her underthings and her cheap, thrilling, paperback novels. She is hungry, for food and more than food. She buries her face in a book, safe as the ostrich's sand.

This lonely night, she'll check into her first hotel. The bellhop will carry her bags, at his insistence, her hand trembling as she searches the coin purse for just the right coin. Hesitating — *Canadian or American? I forget where I am.* Alone in the room, she'll turn the lock till it clicks, slide the gold chain over the bar. But it is not safe yet. There is no fire, no mother whipping cream or popping corn, no assemblage of siblings vying to tell their stories. She'll push the bureau in front of the door, surprising herself with strength she didn't know she possessed. And in front of the bureau, the oblong coffee table, and in front of the coffee table, the honey-wood plant stand and the cherry-wood chair. Now the man with the red coat, wherever he is, cannot reach her.

Satisfied, she'll sprawl on the bed and open her small grocery sack, her purchase from the corner market she had glimpsed while departing the train. "Bananas please, a big bunch of them." The yellow looked so cheerful, so welcoming, and though the man had frightened her, she found herself longing for what he had. *Perhaps no one was either good or bad,* she marveled, which was contrary to all the teachings of her childhood. Each banana she'll peel, then slowly devour, their gold skins rimming her torso like rays, her face timeless and bright as the sun.

Second Panel

June's sister Ruth, who has come here before her, works as a teller at the Broadway First American Bank. There is also another girl — a roommate named Lil — who keeps the same hours, serves the same clientele at their branch. She and Ruth ride the bus together. They are in their 30s — a miraculous thing — neither woman widowed nor wed. June is nearing twenty now. She has a fiancé and a part-time job at the Sears & Roebuck jewelry counter downtown. Her life is unfolding as everyone promised it would.

At home in mid-afternoon, June rushes to prepare supper for the three of them. It is the least she can do. They are letting her stay nearly rent-free, letting her save money for marriage. *This is good practice*, she ponders, foreshadowing her future with Carl. She melts butter in the pan, the way her mother would, then slices onions, presses garlic, waits for these to sizzle, adds the meat. All the while, she has the phonograph on high, the trumpets blaring. These are dark times, she knows, and dark times call for lively music. In her stocking feet on the scrubbed floor, she keeps time.

Standing at the window, daydreaming, the oversized apron falling slack on her thin frame, June forgets about the meat, forgets about the dinner napkins waiting to be pressed, the silverware in need of a quick shine. So the liver or the steak or the white fish or the pink fish turns tough in the pan. "Well done," Ruth always remarks, and June knows it is not a compliment.

Every day is the same: the skillet scarred anew with black char. June remembers what her mother, who served eleven, said—*apples can save anything*. She reaches for the wood bowl, the red and gold bounty Lil carries home from the fruit stand. It's true. The acid from the apples heals all wounds. She scours the pan, then sets the apples to bake for hours. Dessert is a scoop of vanilla ice cream, garnished with hot apple slices, slick with cinnamon and brown sugar. Then, Ruth smiles. Then, Ruth assures her: "Carl is a lucky man."

But not so lucky, it seems. Flying out to his family's house in Minnesota, just weeks before they are to be wed, the plane goes down in a blizzard. June doesn't believe the voice on the phone, wraps the cord around her finger, uncoils it, sinks to her knees. *Not even a widow then*, she thinks, reaching for a word there is no word for.

Ruth makes apple sauce and feeds it to her sister in bed.

Not quite a mother—not quite her mother's voice, not quite her mother's hands. "It is a terrible loss," Ruth says, "but you'll go on."

"How do you know I will?"

"Because you must," Ruth replies. "Because we do."

Lil's shadow appears at the threshold. "Would you like your music?" she asks. "I thought it might soothe you to hear some of the old, familiar tunes."

June shakes her head, the future now a sheet of snow without footprints, a Christmas Eve without carolers. "Leave it off, please," she says.

Third Panel

When June marries John eight years later, they take the train in winter to Montana. "You won't believe the snow here," he promises, kissing her hand. "You've never seen anything like it."

They are married shortly before the War, and their children are born in 1942 and 1945—a new beginning for all of them. His company loans him a car for covering the Great Plains and the Midwest on business. In the meantime, she is left stranded—the bank, supermarket, and post office all several miles away. On the bare roads and back streets of Butte, Montana, June straps the children into their seats, murmurs a quiet prayer, then guides John's lumbering Buick down the drive. On the bare roads and back streets, she teaches herself to drive.

"Why should I always ask Edith for a ride?" she ponders. "If Edith can drive, so can I."

"I have news," June tells him, pouring a cup of coffee, watching as John tucks the triangle of his freshly pressed napkin into his collar. *He doesn't notice*, she observes. *He doesn't care about the creases.*

"Funny," John smiles. "I have news, too. You first."

June reaches for her purse and places before him, beside the shiny silverware, a laminate card with her picture on it. "My license," she proudly declares. "In all the states, I'm legal to drive."

"I see." He lifts it in his hand, turns it over. "Not a forgery?" She shakes her head.

"You didn't have to do anything . . . *improper?*"

"Johnny!" Her face crimsons at the thought.

"Well, you are—as ever—a woman of surprises." He studies her with his wide blue eyes, as if seeing her for the first time. "Well done," John murmurs finally, and she takes it as a compliment.

"So what's your news?"

"I'm taking the family to California for Christmas!" he announces, using his deep radio announcer's voice.

"California!" Bill shouts from the other room. "Really, Dad? *California?*"

"I thought we'd had enough of this cold, and the company's giving me two weeks' paid vacation time." He stands up now and slides his arms around her waist.

"Not in front of the children," June shoos, stepping away.

"Daddy, are we going to Disneyland?" Linda asks, appearing in the doorway.

"We're going *everywhere*. I even picked up a brochure for the Palm Court Hotel."

June turns her back and stands at the stove. "How are we getting there, John?"

"Well, we'll fly of course. Wouldn't you love that, kids? Taking an airplane?"

"*I* wouldn't," June says.

"Mom, it'll be a great adventure," Bill assures, tugging her apron's taut bow.

"I'd prefer not to fly," she replies.

Now a hush falls, broken only by the clatter of plates as she lifts them down from the shelf. "All right . . ." John recovers slowly, "so we'll drive. We'll drive all the way to the land of orange trees. And when we get there, we're going to pick our oranges and pierce them with straws and drink orange juice fresh from the fruit. How does that sound?"

"You can drink orange juice from oranges?" Linda inquires. "I thought it came from a bottle."

"June, do you hear this? Think how we've deprived our children! They think orange juice comes from a bottle!"

Discreetly, she wipes the tears from her eyes, pivots to face them all. "California, here we come." Moving toward him now, taking his hands: "And maybe," June says, "you'll see fit to let me drive some."

Three Keys

After rock comes paper, then scissors: first a soft sheet covering, then the sharp blades slicing away. *Is there sleep in the womb?* I wonder. *Can we sleep in the midst of a dream?* And I am dreaming of you, Mother; here in this rocky seascape, this paper slumber. Onion-skinned — these walls that rip as I wake.

•

The journal is bound with black velvet — my first book whose pages are blank, whose lines uncluttered with language. I open it slowly, flexing the spine. I cut my finger on the fine edge, not expecting paper to be so sharp. With my new pen, I begin to document my life: twelve years lined up in rows like vegetables, the deep furrows and darkening soil.

I write angrily about my mother: *She doesn't understand me. She's always telling me what to do, which I guess is normal, but she doesn't respect my space. . . . No privacy. . . . She comes in when I'm taking a bath. . . . She won't let me shave my legs. . . . Sometimes she screams for no reason. . . . Dad says she has a "hormone problem," whatever that means. It has to do with her hysterectomy. So what? So they cut out some cancer. She should*

25

be happy. Instead, she's cross. She always gets migraines. She makes me wear lipstick and won't let me do my own hair.

•

The tumor begins small, agate of imperceptible ache. It wallows. Its stone-tongue laps at the shore. And here in the shallows beside it, my beginning body is formed. Pink, as a held breath, heart pumping hard, clam-face clenched in its shell. We pass each other, rock over paper, in the elegant amnion sea.

•

My father cooks hot dogs and runny eggs, all he has learned to prepare. I fill the white bowl to the brim with water; he steadies my hands as the excess spills from the sides. We cut open the pack of cellophaned franks, ten skinny sticks of red. "Let's boil 'em till they split open," he says. I gaze at the microwave, our miracle box, the hunger thick on my tongue.

•

"How long?" the doctor inquires.

"Four years." I hear her voice, its thickening gristle of shame.

"Since you were married?"

She shakes her head. "Since we started trying. We wanted to wait awhile. Now it seems we've waited too long."

"You were thirty-three on your last birthday, yes?"

"Yes." *Thickening.*

He sighs onto his stethoscope, cold circle silver against the white lapel of his coat. "Let's run some tests, see what we can find out."

•

In the kitchen, I wash dishes with my father. Our hands prune up, pucker at the knuckles and the wrinkled paths through our palms. *Seventeen, fifty-four*—age does not account for everything. Already the hair under my collar is turning, silver at its roots; his head shimmers the same.

"Jet-black to snow-white before I was thirty. Go figure," he sighs.

Upstairs, my mother is breaking things. Her shoes lose heels, her purses straps. Doors slam. Long after, their knobs still rattle like nervous teeth.

"You can go to hell, both of you! After everything I've done for you, and this is how I'm repaid!"

"It'll pass," my father promises. "It always does." We pass plates between our steamy fingers.

•

"You're pregnant." The doctor's lips hardly move as he hands her the delicate verdict.

"Pregnant? You're certain this time?" She studies his grim ventriloquist's smile.

"Yes, quite certain. We've noticed an *irregularity*, though."

"With the child?" Her heart thuds, earthquake under the water.

"No, not with the child, with the surrounding tissue—the uterine lining. Linda, not to alarm you, but there is an additional growth."

She thickens, water to ice.

•

"Pick your flowers," my father said. "Something tasteful—daisies or daffodils."

Before my eyes, he was turning to stone.

"I like blue ones," I said. "What about carnations? They can turn any color. We can dye them at home."

"There isn't time," he said. "We have to be there in less than an hour."

Looking up now, schoolbag slung over my shoulder: "It's not till tonight, Dad," thinking of my party, my thirteenth birthday. "I'm still not entirely sure what the flowers are for."

We study each other in the shiny light of the flower shop, windows reflecting the bright autumn sun. "Didn't your mother tell you? She sent me to pick you up from school. I thought you—"

"Nobody said anything. They just told me to take my math book. We're starting pre-algebra today."

He laid a large, soft hand on my shoulder. "It's your grandmother's funeral. She died on Thursday. I'm sorry. I thought you knew."

"Not Grandma June!"—thinking of my Upwords partner, her papyrus skin and slender hands, the shawl slipping down from her shoulder.

"No, no, your *mother's mother*. . . . They took out everything, but they still couldn't save her." My father had tears in his eyes, unfolding his handkerchief. "We're so lucky," he said, wiping his face. "It was the same cancer that almost killed your mother."

•

Was there morning, was there evening, the first month? (*the second? the third?*) Darkness—each thumbprint, each pulse of a day—always pressing me down. Even the stone darkens, purples like veins in her thighs.

"*Varicose*," she tells me, lamenting.

"*Spider*," I say, my small finger stroking.

A blue blossom-web explodes.

•

I drop my plate. Between the sink and the cupboard, I let it slide—listen for the grateful break. Nothing. Small square of carpet, and the blue disc my father bends to reclaim.

"It's ok," he says. "It happens to the best of us." Back to the dishpan, smooth porcelain round still soaking.

"Why don't you divorce her?" His eyes flash. "I mean it. Why don't you *fucking* divorce her?"

He hands me the dish again. His face a stone, unchiseled. "I'm going to pretend you never said that."

This time, more purposeful: I throw it down. This time, I aim for the floor.

•

I am negative three months old, my existence disputed for half of a year. *Am I dangerous? Am I too much to bear?* I kick my mother. I warn her: *Yes, I am coming. I will not recede.* My white moon waxes under her skin, stretching and stretching. Now the rock on her hand hardens; each finger breaches and swells. Soon she removes it, bright stone brooding on the vanity mirror. One day, playing dress up, I will slip it over my thumb, then watch as it slides down the drain.

•

"The labor could be difficult, but the child is strong." Dr. Scott's smile is clipped like his tie.

"This is all my husband and I have ever wanted," she tells him plainly. "*Children.* To make our house a home. We bought it cheap, renovated ourselves. Three empty bedrooms to fill."

He nods. "I can help you fill one of them."

"And afterwards?"

"When you're strong enough, we'll talk about surgery."

"Removing the tumor?"

His eyes moist, his voice tight. "At least that, and possibly more."

•

"What is this?" my mother asks. But we both know that's not the real question. She clenches my journal in her strong hands, blocks the doorway at my attempt to adjourn.

"It's mine," I say. "Give it back. What are you doing with it anyway?"

"You left it out on the table, and I thought—since you like to write so much—it must be written like a story. I was going to take it over to your grandma's for tea. I thought we could read it together. But it's a good thing I looked before you embarrassed me in front of your own grandmother."

"I can write whatever I want in my journal."

"Not if it's slander you can't."

I stop. I haven't heard of slander before. Cautiously—"What do you mean?"

"I mean that you aren't allowed to write lies about people. I could take you to court. I could *sue* you."

"I didn't write lies about you." We are the same height now, and I surpassing. We stare into each other's eyes—dark blue, diligent. We gauge each other.

"Cut out those pages. You can write what you want, but I won't have slander in my house, certainly not from my own daughter."

That night over the soap dish, I set my words on fire.

•

Rubbing against it. My jellyfish skin, my wrinkled, translucent fins. The rock hangs heavy beside me: a fractured likeness, a darkly blemished twin. Mother gives in to weariness, plays the piano, hours on end. Show tunes and church hymns, all that she knows—"Easter Parade," "I'm Looking Over a Four-Leaf Clover," "Were You There When They Crucified My Lord?" Sometimes she sings. The dark stone sinks, then rises. I rock since I cannot swim.

•

I drive my father's car to my first apartment—two hours of freeway bordered by spruce and fir. My parents follow. The green seems endless—a lucid dream—until at last, from a side view, I glimpse the delicate furrows of blue. They drive the U-Haul, switching lanes when I do. Water and sky merge at the wavering horizon line. I want to swim through to the clouds.

•

There on the silver table, laced with cotton and gauze, they split her open. I imagine them, the cunning intruders, sharp knives raised in the air. There are the slim margins to think of, the smooth perforation desired. They go in. They enter. Her skin parts softly; her dark blood pools. *Uterus, ovaries, fallopian tubes.* They touch without feeling: the first place setting, the final supper. At the end, one tray is taken out of the room— leftovers thrown away.

•

My parents arrive, steering the steel box, bickering how best to unload. My mother has a vision, she tells us. She's known since she first saw my apartment how it will look when we're done. "There's a right way to do things," she says. "Fortunately, I know the way."

They stay five days. I eat little, sleep less. Each morning I go out for a while. I walk the long streets, graveled and unfamiliar. I enjoy the feeling of being anonymous, this once. Sometimes I still attempt prayer: *God, please make them go away.*

When I return, a locksmith is leaving. There are three silver keys on the chair.

My mother smiles. She holds them up. "See? One for each of us."

•

In the photograph, I pose on the countertop, legs dangling and a glimpse of my jelly shoes. Two years old and smiling. At my ear is the telephone, bright yellow to match the linoleum, receiver turned upside down.

"Who are you talking to?" my father asks.

I look up at the camera flash, his wide hands rimming the lens.

"Mommy," I say.

"That's right. Mommy's in the hospital, but she'll be coming home soon."

Three weeks later, she returns: all carapace and clammy hands.

•

I run through the neighborhood, old streets I have always known. Fifteen and frantic. The stone in my chest jostles and falls. My footsteps thud in my ears. Behind me is my father, following in his car, honking the horn, leaning his gray, weathered head from the window.

"Your mother means well," he shouts. "She's had a bad week."

"She's had a bad *year!*"

"You're all she has left in the world!"

I choke in the cold air. I keep running. We both know I'm bound to come home.

•

It is Tuesday, September 4, 1979—the day after Labor Day at the sweltering summer's end. She wakes to backache, clenching her knees, then raising her hips off the bed.

"Bill, I can't breathe," she says. His sleep shatters: fist through a glass of light.

There is morning, there is evening, the last day. Three trips to the hospital—each time they send her away. My father drives, his thick hands gripping the wheel. She lies back in the seat. She tries to relax—Lamaze class a distant flash. *Take a deep breath, then exhale slowly. That's it. One two three. One two three. Almost like music. Almost like dancing.* She forgets to breathe. She clenches. She screams. Wednesday they give her a room.

•

After the funeral, I stand a long time in my parents' backyard. September has arrived with its pageantry of leaves, soft rustlings and garish pigmentations. Soon, my father will cut the grass for the last time this season. Preparing for hibernation, the way the body does, but my mother's roses will thrive awhile longer.

Around the side of the house I follow the trellis, white

against red brick, tangled with climbing vines and a pastel assortment of flowers. At the fence, I stop to contemplate the free-standing roses, their round faces and exquisite perfumes. Joy and I had always meant to bottle them, having learned that "rose-water" was a delicacy made by steeping or distilling the season's most fragrant petals, a preparation which could be used in both cosmetics and cookery. *Maybe next year,* we promised each other. *Maybe next year,* we promised ourselves.

When I was small and wanted to feel close to her—to the woman in the window with the kerchief on her head, dark hair sheaved with cotton—I would wander in this garden, sampling her flowers, biting in, chewing hard, swallowing: her marigolds, her peonies, her sweet hibiscus and bachelor buttons. *How many calories are in a rose?* I wonder. I half-believe it might be possible: that the red rose, once ingested, will bleed through against my white skin, transforming me into some version of what we had read in class: Shakespeare's sonnet with those roses "damask'd, red and white."

So I am in her garden now— as I must be—quietly, characteristically, feeding at the trough of roses.

•

Her body breaks—china in a closet, an antique vase: hard, cold, irreplaceable. She has been sobbing for thirty-six hours.

My father pleads with the doctor: "Can't you put her out, or under—whatever they say? I can't stand to see her this way."

She is beautiful on the inside. *Soft. Warm.* I want to linger. I decide to remain. But here in the darkness, everything is temporal; everything is fluid.

There also, of course, but I don't expect it somehow—to be forced out of hiding, culled into light.

"You know what they say about Wednesday's child," the doctor reminds her: smiling, seeking to lessen the blow.

My story in limbo, my dark die cast.

She sleeps. I am dragged from a dream.

Triptych of My Mother, Thwarted Thespian, Auditioning for the Part of Her Life

First Panel

She must have seemed a shoo-in for them, cast in the carpenter's family, firstborn of the mute depressive with the broad able hands, firstborn of his cunning, chattering bride, bent on prime real estate and social advancement. Soon, the sister came, followed by the brother, golden-haired cherubs by whose peachy glow she paled in comparison. Linda—of the plain brown hair, the clean white face—so ordinary and attentive, so easy to upstage.

In the kitchen, their mother rattles the silverware drawer—familiar caveat: one missed mark or failed cue will incur thrashing with a wooden spoon or metal spatula. Sharon is gutsy, a rose in full bloom, while Linda's petals turn inward like her toes.

They are playing where the mother told them not to, skating across the freshly shined floor. Linda wants to stop, but Sharon insists. Her figure-eight lands her face down on the spotless linoleum—snap like a tree branch—her pert nose broken so she can barely breathe. "You were supposed to be watching!" the mother shrieks. Sharon bleeds while Linda takes her beating.

Enter the brother with his myriad curls, ringlets fit for the proudest of girls. They dress him up in doll clothes, push him around in a buggy lined with gingham and lace. The father, staring blankly at the television set, observes his son in mauve, bonnet and frock, and his rarely heard voice rears in rage: "Get those Goddamn clothes off of him! No son of mine's gonna grow up to be a queer!"

The same day, Steve's head is shaved. Linda kneels to sweep up the curls. Her mother, kicking the dust pan closer: "You needn't bother getting up."

As she takes her lashes, skirt raised and panties rolled down, Linda listens to her mother's mantra—*You should have known better, known better. . . .* What she knows now is there is no escaping pain, no trellis to climb down or window to slip through, no door that will magically appear. What she knows now is there are only two kinds of pain—the kind you inflict and the kind you endure. At the next casting call, she will stand in a new line, shoulders pushed back and modest chest heaved, auditioning for another role.

Second Panel

By candlelight on an August night, 1967, she accepts the part of wife, promises to play it fully, *for richer or poorer, in sickness and health.* As is the custom, they exchange vows and bands, but she begins already to resent this false equanimity, this pantomime of give and take. So much has been taken from her already, and now he'll have more—her skirt raised, her panties rolled down—and so the litany grows: her finger ringed, her body infiltrated, even her name, such as it was, surrendered.

The husband is a good man, a beacon of well-intentioned oblivion wrapped in a crisp suit, a pair of precisely shined shoes. *He hasn't hurt enough,* she ponders. *Pain is just a shadow for him, a silhouette of someone else's sorrow.* She too becomes a cunning, chattering bride, bent on prime real estate and social advancement. They buy a house on a hill overlooking the Sound, which pleases her somehow: this little trick of language, this confluence of vision and blare.

For a while, the husband disappears into the Air Force. She enjoys her performance of loneliness, scripting letters at an antique escritoire, sealing each envelope with the press of her full red lips; for emphasis, printing S-W-A-K beneath them. *Love*, she thinks, *is safer at a distance.* She sets her wedding album on the coffee table for guests to admire, then casually peruses it the way the audience at a play reviews the program of a show they've seen before. When the outcome is familiar, the theater evolves—a place to *be seen*—the entr'acte and intermission surpassing in exhibition the meager displays of the stage.

It is this spectacle she craves, with her rhinestones and her red leather bag, her appearance in a crowd determined to diminish others. At church, she nominates herself for president of the Men's Group, attends the weekly pancake breakfast, perfumes herself to pungency and relentlessly bats her eyes. She has learned to coax the spotlight in her direction, to cozy up to the gaffers and guide the sponsors smoothly toward her hip pocket where, should they later begin to squirm, she will hold them by their linchpins, poised to comply; otherwise—to suffocate them promptly into silence.

Third Panel
This world is her oyster. This daughter she demands is the pearl. What supper would be complete without a garnish, what lapel without a broach? When the baby comes—despite the growing tumors and the doctor's caveat—she gleams triumphant. *Let them try to short-change her, let them dare!* This child of the plain brown hair, the clean white face, dressed in doll clothes and paraded around in a buggy lined with gingham and lace. *Nearly a blank slate*, the mother marvels, heating the curling iron, pinning the corpulent bows. Begin the acting lessons, the walls plastered with stage directions for a Mamet play, disguised as one of Neil Simon's.

Linda becomes a controversial actress. Some attend her performance out of morbid curiosity, anxious to see what she'll do next. The husband recedes to the wings, slowly accepting that he has become the *man* in *mannequin*, a figure against which other forms are measured, a structure without a speaking part. The daughter, however, will take center stage. She will learn to pirouette and pas de deux, to curtsy on command. The mother, you see, is also the director. She sits in a cross-hatch chair wearing a black beret and chewing the blunt end of a pencil. In a pinch, she will also conduct the orchestra and fire gunshots enlisted for special effect. She likes the feel of a pistol in her hand, stroking the silver slide, the grip made of mother of pearl. Even such props impress her, metonyms of a monstrous power.

If you poll the audience, they will say they thought it intentional, some even gimmicky, the way the dark clouds rolled in and the ashes rained down that day. *Dramatic irony*, most would concede, for the onlookers had come to expect a tragedy. A Sunday morning in May, 1980. A plain white mountain in the Cascade Range: so ordinary before that hour, so easy to upstage. . . .

When Mount St. Helens erupted, some might have called it *too blatant a symbol*, this perfect illustration of bottled rage, too long contained, the physical manifestation of flipping one's lid, blowing one's top. For hundreds of miles, that sound—like a cannon blasting off toward the tranquil stratosphere, then ricocheting back toward the earth. The mother and father did not recognize that this incongruous event portended pressures already uncomfortably rising. Instead, they stood out on the back porch, the infant in arms, mistaking the cloud-crust for a spate of silver linings.

Skin

. . . for the roses
Had the look of flowers that are looked at.

—T. S. Eliot, "Burnt Norton"

First, understand. The body is semiotic, all arrow and ellipsis, the way the garden is potted plant and trailing vine. Sometimes the mind trails behind.

"Your body is a garden," my mother said. She meant that I was a flower. Bend toward the light, please. Take kindly to the camera's shutter and snap. Don't you *shudder and snap* at the strangers, the ones who have come to admire. Bend toward the light, please. Bend toward the men. When the night comes, when the dark—remember to bow your head.

If it was not for skin, I would have thought myself immortal. I had expected any day to sprout wings. What, after all, would bind me to this earth? What roots had I put down, what rhizomes?

Then, without preface, the blossoming began: red rosebuds pushing through the pores. Overnight, a vast acreage of them—radish on a white plate, apple strewn over stucco. This was not the garden she imagined. This was not what the prophesy foretold. Where had they come from? What had I done? Look at me—corsaged or boutonnièred with filthy flowers!

Now I see that *skin* is easy to misspell. We let the *k* slip away to reveal our true intentions. To live in sin is the same as living in skin—the crime of embodiment. We are all guilty, bodied bandits, slaves to our insatiable flesh. But the body, recall, is semiotic. You know the story. When we say, "She had a peaches-and-cream complexion," we mean she was light and good, fair as could be hoped for. When we say, "She had roses in her cheeks," we mean she was tending her garden well: the clear skin, the clean skin, the luminous vision. To have "good skin" is a metonym. It stands in for virtue—piety, purity. To have "bad skin" then—what the doctors call "acne vulgaris"— is to become vulgar yourself, to wear your baser nature on your blemished face, to become an object of dread.

"It is so hard to look at you," she says. I am twelve, approaching thirteen. My mother's eyes are my vanity mirror.

"I never had a blemish a day in my life," she boasts. We sit at the table, buttering our bread.

"Now your father—he was . . . as they say . . . a *pizza face.*"

I look at him and realize we have stopped seeing each other. My mother is the prism through which both of us regard the world.

"It's true," he admits. His voice is low and soft, like a convict at forced confession. "Both my sister and I—it took years to overcome. So many hours under the sun lamp."

"Your sister never *did* overcome it, did she? What a shame." My mother's tone conveys, not sympathy, but muted malice. Aunt Linda, she intimates, is the one who should be ashamed.

"Look closely at Linda's face sometime," my mother instructs. "Notice the cover-up. Skin should be smooth. Hers is gravel— bumps and ridges everywhere, like an unpaved parking lot."

At night, in bed, I can feel the contagion spread. Weeds overtaking a garden. Volcanoes turning active under the skin. My body's surface encoded with messages, a script in Braille.

No one's fingers will ever attempt to decipher me. The code I am will be left forever uncracked. I close my eyes and rehearse the truth of my untouchable body, which I have scrubbed raw with a nail brush, burned bright with blue astringent on a cotton ball. Aunt Linda is a lonely virgin, and my mother explains: "No one wants a blemished bride." Janet Laudan, who teaches Sunday school and elementary school and Vacation Bible School—same reason. "She's forty years old, still living at home with her parents. Look at her skin sometime. Then, think of the woman she could have been."

My mother promises not to let me die alone. "Underneath it all, you're still a very pretty girl. No one can see it now, but soon they will."

Have I mentioned yet—and this is important—my mother is a Master Gardener. She heads a garden club and holds a certificate of some kind from the state.

When she speaks, her tongue is a trowel turning over the soil.

"I want you to be polite and look the doctor in the eye. I know you're embarrassed, but acne doesn't exempt you from good manners."

The dermatologist is old and striking. She has strawberry hair flecked with gray, smooth milky skin, and a smattering of freckles.

"That's surprising," my mother later remarks. "You'd think, in her line of work, she could have had those little dots erased."

When Rose Kennedy examines me, she begins with my face. I lie down on the crinkly paper and gaze up into her massive monocle. More like a magnifying glass, which she can maneuver readily on its adjustable metal bar. With this lens, she will look through me—down through the epidermis and the dermis to my subcutaneous soul.

"Can it be fixed?" my mother pesters every few moments.

Next, I must remove my shirt, my white cotton training

bra with its pink rosette at the center cross. I press my new breasts into the white tissue paper, afraid of what she will say, anticipating the soft gasp when she sees me for what I really am. I feel like a present freshly unwrapped, certain I am about to be sent back.

"This is something," Dr. Kennedy says.

My mother, troweling behind her: "Can it be fixed?"

"Well, certainly she does have a severe case of acne, which we *can* treat, but I'm a bit more concerned about these moles." Her fingers are cool, but my skin warms to her touch. *Is this like what happens to boys?* I wonder.

"What about them?"

"Has she always had them? Have you ever noticed any changes in them?"

"Not that I can say, no. Is there a problem?"

"I'd like to do some measurements, take a couple of pictures, keep a record of the moles. It may be nothing, or it may be that we need to remove one or more of them—if they show signs of discoloration or changing shape or—"

"Worst-case scenario: would it leave a scar?"

"Yes," Dr. Kennedy says. "A small hole—a divot in the skin. But that's what sometimes has to be done if there is a threat of melanoma."

Later, with my shirt on again, my second pulse no longer thumping, I brace for pain. She holds a small, silver utensil. It is an aesthetic implement, with a space cut out in the shape of a circle. This circle she places over each dark pore. Under the hot lamp, as my father forewarned, she squeezes the buds till they bleed.

Tonight my mother goes to her garden club, so my father and I stay home watering her flowers.

"Your mother has a gift," he reminds me. "She can make anything grow."

"I know." He fills the watering can, and I carry it up to the rockery to lavish the thirsty ferns. "The dermatologist says she might have to remove some of my moles." When he doesn't respond, I have to say something more drastic. "Dr. Kennedy thinks I could get cancer."

"What? Your mother didn't say—"

"She doesn't want to believe it, but Dr. Kennedy is pretty sure. For all we know, I could end up like JoAnne."

The year before, my mother's best friend since junior high school passed away from cancer originating in moles on her back. She had never wanted them removed because she didn't like the idea of looking bad in her bathing suit. A blemish was a blemish, after all.

"Don't say that. Don't you dare! What happened to JoAnne was rare, and if it came to that, we would never do anything to jeopardize your health."

My father is standing below me on the patio in a stained undershirt and dirty brown shorts. These are his "work clothes." He holds the garden hose in one hand and a garbage bag in the other.

"Dr. Kennedy says we could always have the moles removed now—just to be safe. There are only five of them. They can't hurt me if they're not there."

He doesn't ask if that's what I want. Secretly, I am hoping he will. Instead, he wipes his brow with the back of his hand and says, "We'll have to talk to your mother. My guess is she wouldn't want to do anything rash."

"It's not rash," I tell him, feigning confidence. "It's *preventative*."

"*Still*—we'll have to talk to your mother about that."

In my childhood, I never had chicken pox. Though I romped through foliage and dangled from trees, I never contracted poison oak or poison ivy. I had unmarred olive skin—the color of well-creamed coffee—that always tanned and never burned and glowed all summer in a way my Aunt Linda called "radiant" and my father called "brown as a berry," even though there were no brown berries as far as I knew. The consensus had been that, though I wasn't fair, I was smooth and had appeared for so many years unblemished. I had not been, in other words, *a disappointment.*

Then, just when it began to matter, just when I could raise my skirts without scabs on my knees and prepare for boys as more than mere opponents on the playground, this anti-garden, shadow-garden bloomed.

"Do you know what my mother used to say?" my mother said. I shook my head. *Her* mother was steel-eyed and silver-haired and full of rage, always glaring at us from behind the half-drawn eyelet curtains. "She used to say—with acne, that is—that it's the meanness coming out of you."

I, incredulous: "Did you believe her?"

"I didn't have to. Nothing like that was coming out of *me.*"

"Like that" was a euphemism for pus and blood and the dark center of the blackhead that my mother mistook for dirt. Dr. Kennedy had repeatedly explained that a blackhead, known in the medical world as "open comedo"—like something funny, to be alternately scoffed at and ignored—was a blocked pore filled with keratin. "You can't scrub it clean," she insisted. "It isn't dirty."

But the body is semiotic, and the blackhead is a sign. We respond to signs in our world by way of ritual.

Every morning, I went to my mother's bathroom and waited for the ceremonial cleanse. She steamed a wash cloth and pressed it to my face. Then, she lathered it with dermatologist-supplied soap—the kind the pharmacist handed you through the little scooped neck of his window. Everybody knew about my debasement. We scrubbed and rinsed my face three times. Then, the astringent. When my pores stopped stinging, it was time to apply the cream.

Despite our rigor, what we didn't see was improvement. Instead, proliferation: the rough red typography of my face

extending to my scalp, into my ears, blazing down my neck
and fanning out onto my shoulders. Even armpits were not
immune. And my back, which was long and progressively
studded as if with nails, began to itch impossibly under my
shirts and burn beneath the cinch of my belt.

"Have you thought about a different doctor," my father
asked, "someone who favors more aggressive treatment?"

"Of course I've _thought_ about it," my mother snapped.
She speared green beans and held them steady on her fork
like the crenellated wall of a castle. I pictured myself behind
that wall, and nothing short of a catapult would set me free.
"My guess is that all these sissy doctors are the same. They say
it's _common_ in adolescence. They say it's _likely_ to clear up on
its own. They say 85% of teenagers have it to some degree. I
don't believe it. Does that look _normal_ to you?"

Together, they peered at my face across the table.

"No," my mother decreed. "It's time to take matters into
my own hands."

It is fitting, I suppose, that morning matins should be followed by vespers and the evening repose. This gives the day
a certain symmetry, beginning in purge and ending in praise.
So when we cleared our plates from the table, I knew where
I should solemnly proceed. My father would wash the dishes
while my mother would lead me away. "Just remember," he
liked to say, "everything she does is for your own good."

I tried to remember. I am still trying to remember.

The bedroom windows were always open, a sea breeze rus-
tling the opaque curtains. Our astringent was also called Sea
Breeze—an irony that struck me with a poignant punch.
They felt so different on the skin, those two breezes.

"I'd like to leave the windows open," my mother said. "Can
I trust you not to scream?"

I too wanted her to leave the windows open, so I would
promise not to scream.

"You know that if you do scream, I'll have to close the windows. I don't want to, but we can't have the neighbors wondering and getting the wrong idea."

The first position was prone. I think the first position is always prone. We lie the way we are good at, the way we know best. I put my face into my mother's pillow, which always smelled sweet, like one of her many perfumes. She pulled up my shirt, unfastened my bra, and straddled me across my still-narrow hips. The hot wash cloth scalded and soothed at once. Spontaneous tears stung my eyes.

"Ready?" But I didn't have to respond. This was her "picking time." It was her hour, or two, or more, of pure, uninterrupted pleasure. She didn't pick them like flowers, though in a sense they were—flowers resembling weeds in a pocked and poorly irrigated garden. She squeezed them between her thumbnails until they "popped," talking all the while, sometimes evangelizing and other times only gently advising. I learned that I would come through this. I learned that I was not ruined. I learned that my chances were as good as any other girl's, but the sad truth of the world was that people judged us by our appearance, not by the contents of our minds.

Form precedes content, she might have said, and I the sorry sonnet, the villainous villanelle.

Before turning me over, my mother laid down a towel. She didn't want her clean linens stained with my blood. "Wait right there. You're bleeding some—not too bad, but I can't have you oozing all over the sheets!" It was a little joke to her. "It hurts so much worse to have babies. You wouldn't believe. This is really *nothing* compared to that."

As I lay on my back, watching the curtains flutter overhead, I tried to avoid my mother's eyes. She wanted me to agree that this was "in my best interest." She wanted me to concur that I had received a blessing akin to communion itself. After all, she had sacrificed her whole evening—many evenings a week—

every evening she wasn't at garden club—to try to redeem me, to purify my pores and begin to alleviate my terrible, racking, presupposed social embarrassment.

"It makes me want to cry every day when I send you to school this way," she whimpered. "Do the other kids tease you? Don't tell me. I don't think I even want to know."

At the conclusion of our hour, or two, or more, of her pure, uninterrupted pleasure, her delighted exclamations of "that was a *huge* one!" and "I wish you could see how much *pus* I've wiped away!", there was a final act of passion to be performed. Think of the double meaning of this word. Passion, for her, as in zeal. Passion, for me, as in suffering. A cool washcloth, to "close up" the pores. And then the astringent, to make sure they were sealed tight for the rest of the night.

Here is where I would plead: "Not the astringent! Please! No Sea Breeze!"

"If I don't do it, everything else I have done tonight will be for naught. Is that what you want?"

"No." But I was weeping, and she was threatening to close the windows.

"Then let me do it. It isn't going to hurt that bad."

"But it is! But it is! I know because it always does!"

The pain went through me. I felt it pass from the epidermis through the dermis, all the way to my subcutaneous soul. I tried to rise up above it and look down, as if through a massive monocle, a magnifying glass. But then I remembered how my friend April once showed me the way magnifying glasses can direct sunlight toward an ant or beetle, zapping it as if with lightning, striking the creature instantly dead in its tracks.

When it was done, my mother cooed and blew her soft breath all over my face. "There, there. The things we do for beauty. The things we *have* to do." Then, as ritual dictates, she gave her benediction. She told me to clean myself up and hurry downstairs, where there was rainbow sherbet waiting for me. "I know," she said, "how much you like ice cream."

The summer before high school begins, I fall prey to unexpected permutations. First, my mother selects a new dermatologist. Second, or simultaneously, I fall in love with someone on television.

Brandith Irwin is young, thin, spectacled, and austere, but she does have impeccable ivory skin. I have seen her picture on the Madison Avenue dermatology bulletin board. She also has a husband, who is a lawyer, and a son, who will never have to worry about acne vulgaris, or anything else for that matter. Of this my mother is sure.

"I think you're going to like her," my mother says, sifting through a waiting room magazine. "In fact, you may want to interview her for that job-shadowing program at school. Remember: you'll have to think ahead for sophomore year."

"Why would I want to do that—interview Dr. Irwin, I mean?"

"All these years we've tried to encourage you to pursue pediatrics, but dermatology would be fine, too. You could help young girls just like yourself, girls who thought everything was hopeless until they walked into Dr. *Wade's* office." She nudges me with an elbow to the ribs.

"I'm not interested in being a doctor, Mom. You know I want to be a private eye."

"This is neither the time nor place to rehash that discussion, but I am going to *request* that you not embarrass me today and further, that you give some serious thought to what Dr. Irwin could do for you—beyond your immediate problem."

In her office, I make a sudden resolution. I will not speak, even when directly addressed. If my mother is so bent on my submission, why should I use my voice at all? I am fourteen now, fated to scrutiny and dissatisfaction. Silence is my only revenge.

"Hi Julie, I'm Dr. Irwin," she says in a serious tone. I shake her hand, meet her eyes, and say nothing. "I see you're here about your acne. Let's have a closer look, shall we? Have a seat up here on this table please."

She removes her own small, wire-rimmed glasses and replaces them with enormous, square-shaped spectacles. There are magnifying lenses inside. I close my eyes during this inspection, practice transporting myself to somewhere else. "Your skin does seem resistant to treatment," she notes. "I'm guessing your previous doctor prescribed topical creams, but I'm going to suggest a new approach."

"Yes, by all means!" my mother exclaims. I can feel her inching closer, and my body bristles. "I've felt all along that the soap and the Retin-A weren't really strong enough. I knew there had to be a better way."

"And the acne—is it anywhere else on her body?" Dr. Irwin is no longer speaking to me.

"Yes, it's everywhere! It's *epidemic*—scalp, ears, neck, back, shoulders. She sweats so much—far too much for a girl, I think, which may be part of the problem."

"Well, she does have naturally oily skin, and my guess is that it's become much worse since the onset of puberty."

My mother feels validated now. "That's right. We were going along just fine, and I had this lovely, clear-skinned daughter, and then one day—her pores just erupted. Nothing but pimples and grease."

No one has noticed that I have withdrawn. I am no longer speaking, no longer meeting anyone's eyes. My mother and Dr. Irwin chat like long-lost sorority sisters. "I can see that this has been hard on you," Dr. Irwin consoles, still with her flat voice and expressionless face.

"Oh, so difficult, you have no idea! It pains me to take a picture."

"I'm going to recommend two things. The first is a pill called Accutane, which has been shown to do wonders for drying up the skin and with it, the acne. About 80% of patients

find it works successfully after the first round of treatment—
four months—while another 10% need a second round."

"And the final 10%?"

Dr. Irwin is scribbling on a prescription pad. "Unfortunately,
for that population, nothing seems to work. Some patients are
just highly resistant to treatment. But the results with Accutane
have been far better than with any other drug. Also, if you'd
like, I can prescribe something to help with perspiration."

"Oh, I certainly would. You wouldn't believe the number
of shirts she's ruined, the number of clothes I have to soak in
salt to get the odor out, not to mention the yellow stains."

I have crossed my arms. I have adjusted my posture to indi-
cate my displeasure. I want to scream, "Don't you understand
that I'm *ignoring* you? Don't you even *care*?"

"Now the instructions for Drysol are straightforward. Just
read and follow. The Accutane is a bit more complex because
of its history of causing birth defects in children of mothers
who became pregnant while taking the drug. For this reason,
we're going to have to ask Julie to come in on a weekly basis for
a pregnancy test."

"A pregnancy test?" The words escape my lips before I can
restrain them—like a balloon coming loose from a wrist.

"This is purely a precaution, but it is also a legal require-
ment of taking the drug. That is, I can't prescribe it unless you
commit to weekly pregnancy tests."

My mother's face scorches red with indignation. "She's
fourteen years old. She's been raised right. There's no way in
the world—"

"Again, it's not that I don't believe you, but a pregnancy
test is legally required for all female patients taking this drug."

"The things we do for beauty," my mother mutters. "The
things we *have* to do."

My mother and Dr. Irwin strike a bargain then, negotiate the
details, shake hands and kiss each other's rings. They are in
collusion now, and the enemy is not "excessive sebum in the

skin," but something far more potent and difficult to kill—ugliness, undesirability. The body is semiotic, after all. Acne is a metonym. And if no one wants me, if no one can ever be persuaded to want me, think how hard that would be . . . *on my mother.*

When I wake in the morning—before matins, before my mother is even awake, her faucet turned to full heat and her washcloths soaking—I am wrapped in a warm feeling I wish could last forever. In my mind, I am watching a commercial. I know it so well I can play it effortlessly, projected against the interior screen of my eyelids. My father had been taping original James Bond movies onto VHS tapes from television. One of them had caught this commercial as well, preserved it in all its glorious perfection. The tape had then gone missing, much to his chagrin. Slowly, I extend my hand to the stash of books beneath my nightstand, and there, in the far back, wedged between the carpet and the wall, I feel it—the hard plastic with two inset wheels. My pulse thumps a little at the prospect.

The girl's name is Rebecca Gayheart. I have learned this through the computers at school. Her name, like her face, is smooth and soft and desirable—my little mantra, safe to repeat in the dark: *Rebecca Gayheart. Rebecca Gayheart.* She has full lips and thick curls and blue eyes and, yes, it's true, roses in her cheeks. The commercial, strangely, is for a face cream. She is worried that the boy at school who has asked her for a date will be horrified when he sees the acne on her face. (I have paused the tape and watched it frame by frame; there is no acne, or trace of acne, on her face.) Then, the voiceover says, "Relax, you wash every time, every day, with Noxzema." She stands in the bathroom, no mother supervising, her hair pulled back in one of those breezy ponytails, her arms bare and breasts free in a loose tank top and drawstring pajama bottoms.

She lathers her skin with the contents of the magic blue jar, then easily splashes the white foam away. When she sees the boy, he tells her how great she looks, and she blushes because she knows it's true. He is about to kiss her at the commercial's close, and of course she wants him to. But in my version, *I* tell her how she really looks great. *I'm* the one who asks her out for a date. She smiles at me, doesn't think it's strange, leans in closer—so close I can feel her breath on my face. She puts her finger in my dimple and kisses my cheek. I open my mouth to kiss her back. This is a reflex, like the doctor striking my knee and my knee bouncing. It will be a big kiss—the first one that matters, with tongue and everything—and I am trembling, half-asleep, half-awake, and then, invariably, my mother's voice cuts in—"Julie! Bathroom! I haven't got all day!"

Gradually, my skin begins to reflect the effects of Accutane. It will take two rounds with me, Dr. Irwin is sure, but at the end of eight months, I'll hardly be the same person anymore. "Just in time for spring tolo," my mother grins. "Be thinking ahead about who you'd like to bring."

"Mom, I think I'd like to get some Noxzema," I say, trying to sound casual. If she senses it's important to me, she'll try to take advantage, see what she can get in exchange.

"Some *what*?" She is barely listening as she wields her shopping cart down the aisle.

"You know—there are commercials for it on television. It's a face cream. It's good for your skin. It's . . . *preventative*, so the pimples won't come back."

"It's over the counter?"

"Yes. They sell it everywhere—drug stores, grocery stores. We could get it here."

"Why would we do that when your father's insurance pays for prescription soap?"

I shrug, holding my ground, pushing my anger deep down. "It couldn't hurt. Even as a backup. I have my own money."

"No," my mother vetoes. "It isn't in Dr. Irwin's plan. We have to stick to her plan."

Now the anger begins to vaporize, to rise off my skin like

steam. "Well, you picking my face isn't in Dr. Irwin's plan either. She doesn't even know you're doing it, and I'm pretty sure she wouldn't approve."

My mother shudders and snaps to attention, there among the milk and eggs, there with the cold breezes blowing. "Are you attempting to . . . *blackmail* me?" She sounds like a villain in a movie, the way she draws the words out for emphasis, her lip curling in an unctuous way.

"No. I'm just pointing out that my skin is drying up now, and there aren't nearly as many pimples as before, but you're still picking them."

"And you think you're going to *deprive* me of that? You think you're going to tell Dr. Irwin and get your mother in trouble?" Her teeth are streaked red with lipstick. Her hair is dyed red with L'Oréal. "After all I've done for you through this whole ordeal. . . ."

"Mom, I just want some Noxzema."

"And I just want a grateful daughter. So I guess neither of us is going to get what she wants."

That night, she shows no mercy. I bleed and bleed. The astringent sears my skin until I scream, and my mother closes the windows and slaps my thighs and doesn't offer me ice cream, or sherbet, which is not really ice cream, and even the thought of kissing Rebecca Gayheart isn't enough to ease the pain.

They call a callus a "wound response," or at least I have heard it described that way. A callus forms when a small area of skin becomes hard and thick, usually as a result of prolonged pressure or friction. Acne, it turns out, can also be caused by stress, which is prolonged pressure or friction of a distinctly psychological kind. The skin, while also an organ, while also a living thing in a constant state of regeneration, is also a metaphor. To be "thin-skinned" means to be vulnerable. People have the power to hurt you—with a gesture, a word, a touch, or a refusal to touch. But to be "thick-skinned" is another way of saying "emotionally callused." Touch me where I'm callused, and watch how I won't respond. It isn't malice or pretension. It's only the dead nerve cells that have fallen away, leaving a numb part, a place without feeling.

My fourteen-year-old self was a romantic. She still believed love was a pumice, though pumice is also a stone. She knew there were hard places in all of us, that she was simply no exception to the rule.

"Oh look! Your shoulders are finally clear enough to wear a strapless dress!" It is white and soft and shows the nape of my neck and the pert fins in my back and the little trail of dark brown moles—all five of them—leading somewhere perhaps, or nowhere at all.

"Now be sure to put your Drysol on extra tonight. I don't want you ruining this dress."

"But I just shaved under my arms. You're not supposed to apply it to newly shaved skin."

"Do you want to have huge perspiration circles while you're dancing? Do you want to make a spectacle out of yourself?"

In the bathroom, I apply the Drysol that seals up my pores, making it impossible to perspire. My armpits like corked water jugs, bloated and aching. Tonight the raw skin burns like Sea Breeze on fresh wounds, the razed garden of my skin after picking season. I can hardly lift my arms to place them on Karl Erickson's shoulders. We are just in time for the first slow dance.

Bone

I always had "good bones," the doctor said, tapping my knee with his tiny hammer. "Fine bone structure," it was clear to see, like my mother, who—by her own estimation— was still beautiful despite her large bones. "But women like us," she said, "we have to work a little harder."

Women like us. I swallowed the words. *What kind of women were we?* I attempted the math. *How many kinds of women could there be?*

I had been dancing with Katy Parker since kindergarten. There was nothing plush about her, nothing soft. Her body an x-ray of itself—the bones always showing, always poking through like nails in plaster, with a face blank and bare, as if someone had forgotten to hang a picture. Small and flexible, she slid down easily into the splits; strong and confident, she rose up easily onto her toes, pirouette after pirouette, followed by the perfect curtsy.

I could not dance. I moved awkwardly through the motions, body at a distance, a thing to be reckoned with, separate from myself. They kept me in the chorus mostly, in the back because I was tall—a choreographer's ready-made alibi. It didn't matter about the spotlight. I didn't want to be showcased; I knew I had nothing to show. But at the end of each night, each performance on the Chief Sealth High School stage, Katy's parents brought her roses. She held them in her arms like a newborn baby, rocking them, the green tissue paper drawn back so strangers could see their pretty faces, red and pink and golden. The fragrance filled the dressing room. Other girls gathered around to admire.

When I mentioned it once to my mother—this spectacle of roses—she said only, "What do you need cut flowers for? You have a whole garden waiting for you at home."

It was after dress rehearsal, one of those nights in late spring, that an idea came to me, washed up on the shore of my mind like a note in a barnacled bottle. My grandma and Aunt Linda sat patiently in the auditorium. They praised me effusively on the car ride home. Then, my grandmother said, "You know, Linda used to dance ballet. It lasted until she was twelve or thirteen. She wanted to get her pointe shoes. She wanted to dance in *Swan Lake*."

"Did you?" I asked, thinking of the pink ribbons that older girls braided around their calves, bodies like a Maypole on the day of celebration.

"No," she replied. "It turns out that dancing *en pointe* is very painful. Your toes bleed something awful, and it requires a great deal of strength to support yourself that way—something I didn't have."

"Yes, dear. Your aunt was always a delicate girl. She didn't have your . . . *hardiness*. Sometimes, in a windstorm, I thought she would be swept away."

So my aunt was sad because she had *small* bones, *soft* bones, the kind that snapped easily under pressure. She had worn so many casts and slings, endured so many settings and sutures.

She hated being *brittle*, which was a gentle accusation, a euphemism for *deficient* or *weak*.

But I didn't like being called *hardy* either. Certainly, I was. Apart from tutus and leotards and nights on the stage, I was a tomboy, a kickball all-star, the kind of girl who bristled if a boy called her a girl or accused her of playing like one. This didn't mean I wanted girls to call me a boy, to see me as "big-boned" and "masculine," where moxie replaced grace or the possibility of it. Couldn't I have both? Couldn't I dance like a girl and play like a boy and come home with a bouquet of roses in my arms?

The kitchen table was set with white bowls and wooden spoons, and my grandmother asked, "Who wants vanilla with chocolate syrup, and who wants Neapolitan?" There were wafers too, arranged on saucers—pink and yellow and brown—and a pot of coffee percolating on the counter.

"Thanks, Grandma, but I'm really full tonight."

This was my idea.

"Nonsense! You've been dancing for two hours! You must be famished!"

An idea that the body was simply bone shrink-wrapped into certain sizes; that the size could be changed by shrinking the wrap itself, winnowing the skin.

"Oh, it's ok, really. I don't feel like ice cream. My stomach's been a little upset."

"You have the heartiest appetite of any girl I know," my aunt remarked. "It's not like you to turn down ice cream."

"I know," I blushed. "I'm sorry."

In my grandmother's shower, I scrubbed my hair and listened to my stomach rumble. Ten minutes later, turbaned and robed, I sat down at the table and requested my bowl. "I changed my mind," I said. "Neapolitan please—lots of strawberry."

Then, the years of dancing came to an end. I focused on piano instead. "You have long fingers," the instructor said, "long and thin." His observation conveyed approval.

Once, my whole body had been described this way—*long and thin*. Like my father—*a tall drink of water*. But I was a shapeshifter then, jutting out and curving in like a coastline—abruptly bumpy, suddenly ridged. Softer too, so the bones hid under the skin. You had to press hard if you wanted to see them.

"You'll never believe it!" my mother exclaims, bursting in on me in the bath. I pull my knees up to my chest. I clutch my fists under water. "Someone has anonymously nominated you for the Miss Pre-Teen America Pageant!"

"Me?"

"Well, don't look so surprised! There's more to you than meets the eye," she beams, "and this is your chance to prove it."

Skeptically: "What do I have to do?"

She consults the grainy cardstock from the envelope. "First, you have to write an essay explaining why you are a good candidate to be Miss Pre-Teen America—what you have to offer."

"What *do* I have to offer?"

My mother perches on the toilet seat skimming the documents, but when I say this, she looks up at me and scowls. "What do you mean what do you have to offer? *Poise! Confidence! Leadership ability!* You are an *ideal* representative of America's pre-teen girls."

"That's unfortunate," I murmur, thinking of Katy Parker, her taut body of contradictions: strength and grace, power and elegance.

Now my mother sticks her toe in the water and splashes my face. "Am I hearing you right? You've been given the opportunity of a lifetime, and you're making light?"

"Where does it lead? I mean, if I go to this pageant, and I win—"

"*When* you win," she corrects me.

"Then, what happens?"

"Then, you go on to compete for Miss *Teen* America, and

from there—you could become *Miss America!* You could win a scholarship to college and be the envy of every young woman in the country!" From the way she says it, raising these two possibilities like silver platters on her hands, I can't tell which she values more, the scholarship or the capacity to incite envy in others.

"You also have to send a picture and a résumé detailing your accomplishments. That should be easy enough. You've done plenty of extracurricular activities and volunteer work with the church, and as far as the picture goes"—inching her slippers back on her feet—"I think I still have some 4 x 6 glossies from *Yuen Lui.*"

"Those are old pictures," I say. "I'm ten in them."

"You're thinner then—and you don't have acne."

So it happens that around this time, my father and Katy Parker's father decide to go fishing. We have been invited to a barbecue on Camano Island, and Mrs. Parker suggests that Katy and I go out in one of the canoes. "It'll be fun," she says. "Katy's been moping around here all weekend, and I think she could do with a bit of fresh air."

"I'm not in the mood, Mom," she retorts, not looking at me, swinging her braid in a way that indicates displeasure.

"Be that as it may, we have guests, and you've been ignoring everyone all day."

In the boat, Katy eats string cheese and looks bored. She doesn't want to row, so I do my best to guide us away from the shore. In the distance, we can hear our fathers' muted conversation, the splash of her sister and brother throwing rocks into the sea. "Neil! Nora! You better not be doing what I think you're doing!"

"We're not trying to hit Katy!" Neil replies. "I'm teaching Nora how to skip stones."

"He's throwing rocks at us, of course," Katy says. "But he throws like a girl, so don't worry."

I shrug my shoulders. "I wasn't worried."

"My mom says you're starting at a new dance studio in the fall."

"I am? Funny. That's the first I've heard of it."

"Maybe you should join a sports team or something. You'd probably be good."

I intercept her eyes before she can look out at the water again. "Why do you say that? What is it about me that makes you say that?"

"God, don't get so intense," she sighs. "It's just a hunch. You don't seem like you like dancing very much."

"So why do you think I'd like sports instead?" We go to different schools, so she doesn't know I'm tetherball champ three years running or that I can outkick Carl Lull on a good day in kickball.

Katy stretches her legs, which are bruised and bony and smoothly shaved without a scratch or gash. She points and flexes her toes out of habit. "Ok, I'll play. Have you ever seen that wretched movie *Freaky Friday?*"

"Sure."

"Well, I have to watch it like a hundred times a week because of Nora, and—I don't know—you just remind me of the girl in it. Whatever her name is."

"Annabel Andrews?" This is incredible. Annabel Andrews is one of my heroes.

"I hope that doesn't offend you. It's just an observation."

"Why would it offend me? She's awesome! She's such a rebel, not to mention phenomenal on water skis."

"See. There you go. You've got that athletic thing that she has. And you know, at the end, she goes to the beauty salon and starts to look a lot better. That neighbor guy even wants to go out with her."

"But Boris is a doofus," I protest.

"So what? He still wants to go out with her."

There it was. Why hadn't I noticed it before? Part of the equation was making ourselves enviable to other women; the other part was making ourselves desirable to men. I knew this, of course, but I kept forgetting. I kept falling into body amnesia whenever boys were around.

Annabel Andrews states her weight in the opening monologue, then hurriedly mentions that she's "watching it," as if to reassure us. *Of what?* Even though we see her only a few scenes later eating a rum raisin banana split for breakfast — the undeniable lure of ice cream at any time of day — she knows that her body must be closely monitored, the appropriate ratio of bone to skin maintained.

We saw this body awareness other places, too. We saw a trend of women being replaced — in talk show hosts and second marriages. Sometimes, with plastic surgery, women were replacing themselves.

Even on *Roseanne*, a television show I wasn't allowed to watch — a show about "vulgar, overweight people," my mother said — they had upgraded to a different daughter. Becky, the blond one, the archetype of the daughter that I was clearly not, had been replaced by a newer, blonder daughter. They were trying to make her the same, as close as possible to the original, but better if they could. *Thinner.*

Later, I would observe the same trend on a show I was allowed to watch — *Dr. Quinn, Medicine Woman.* When Jessica Bowman replaced Erika Flores as Colleen, they weren't even trying for look-alikes. The blond, bosomy daughter came back from hiatus a rail-thin, dark-haired girl, a Katy Parker. My mother remarked approvingly, "Now there's a switch." Even under the frumpy pioneer dresses, her bones sat straight and small and polished, like a row of good white teeth.

The pageant will take place at a Marriott Hotel in Sea-Tac, Washington, the day of and the day following my thirteenth birthday. As long as you are not yet thirteen when you complete the required paperwork, you are allowed to compete for the Miss Pre-Teen America crown. But I am not so interested in the crown. What keeps me engaged is the prospect of the roses, the pageant-purchased bouquet lavished upon the winner when she walks down the elevated aisle, waving and smiling, Vaseline thick on her teeth, and those roses—long-stemmed with thorns removed—decadently draped on her arm.

I am beginning to spend more time in front of the mirror. My mother says we will "do whatever it takes" to camouflage the blemishes on my face during the days of the pageant. For now, I have a speech to write and a sonatina to memorize, and in general, whenever possible, I should practice walking in my evening gown with high heels and a book balanced carefully on my head.

"Use the Bible," my father says. "It's heavy, and it's a sure sign God will be with you." He laughs at his own joke, but I find it hard these days to even meet his eyes.

I am also eating less and learning to control my hunger. With the first pang, I take a glass of water. With the second, I chew the ice. When my stomach deflates like an empty balloon, it's time to go swimming. A sport of leisure has become a rehearsal of martyrdom. I must *outswim* the hunger now. Twenty laps, forty, sixty. . . . When I get tired, I frog-kick with the board.

My mother looks favorably down from the kitchen window, from the rockery with shears in hand, from the verandah with the small shrubs and hanging baskets. "We have to get our money's worth on that pool," she says. "I bet you're glad we had it built in-ground—none of those blue plastic monstrosities—and a long way from wall to wall."

Look at the story embedded under the words, like an obscure painting with a notorious one preserved beneath. I have heard the word *aesthetic*, meaning "pleasing to the eye." Now I learn its sound-alike word—*ascetic*. A smaller word, thinner. Their resemblance is no accident. The one leads into the other, and the other corroborates it.

Once, that summer, I strayed. The garden club was coming over, but there were fewer guests than my mother had expected. On the stovetop, the lure of leftovers. They were baked goods, from a real bakery with a shiny white box. I had never seen this kind of pastry before, this puffy bread that tapered at the ends, its thin skin that flaked when you touched it. I held one in my hand, felt its paradox of levity and heft.

I ate the first one standing at the window, vigilant, in case someone should see. The second one I gobbled, its taste dissolving on my tongue like a communion wafer, but this one buttery, sweet, a gustatory blessing.

The third one I took to my room and savored. I stretched out on my bed and gazed at the wreath of dried flowers encircling the overhead light. *A bite.* I studied the framed pictures of ballet slippers that adorned the walls, the one crystalline pair that dangled on a pink thread over my mirror. *Another bite: slow, thoughtful.* Who had put those things there? I never chose them. Some of them had always been there, and others seemed to subtly appear—the mobile, the dollhouse, the miniature rocking chair, the little crocheted wall-hanging that read, in pink script, *Girls are sugar and spice and everything nice*, and the plaque, reclining on its tripod, that read, in extravagant gold cursive, *A daughter is a mother's pride, a father's joy . . . their dream come true.* I finished the croissant and fell asleep. When I woke, my mother was seated beside me, her shoulders heaving as she sobbed.

"What is it, Mom? What's wrong?"

"There were three croissants left in the box. Did you eat them?"

"Oh—I thought they were leftovers. I thought they were ours to keep."

"Julie, tell me you saved them, at least two of them. Tell me you didn't eat them all."

She wiped her eye shadow on her apron, which was also blue—a light shift patterned with flowers.

"I'm sorry. I guess I was really hungry."

Her red mouth froze in horror. "So you did—you actually ate them all?"

I nodded. "Do you want me to pay for them?"

"Do you have *any idea* how many calories are in a croissant, how many *fat grams*?"

I shook my head, sitting up now, feeling the acid rise in my throat.

"Julie, I only ate *a fourth* of one. They're so fattening I felt I could only eat *a fourth*! You've eaten three of the most decadent desserts a person could eat!"

"I thought it was bread, just fancy bread. I didn't know it was dessert."

"Get up! You're just lying there with all that fat in your stomach!" She was in a panic now. "No more food for you today! You can have a vegetable at dinner. Go, now, *go*!"

"What should I—"

The tears were streaming down her face faster now, taking her mascara with them in thick, black rivers. "I don't care! Run around the block, for starters. Get in the pool. If there was ever a day for lap swim, today is that day." I am lacing up my tennis shoes, heart pounding loud in my ears. "Do you have a jump rope?"

"Yes—in the garage."

"Some women jump rope to lose weight after giving birth. Go get your jump rope and bring it down to the backyard. Later," she promised, "we'll tap-dance together." We did this sometimes, in the basement, each of us on a piece of plywood, listening to show tunes. It was part of my mother's workout regimen. "What are you waiting for?" she cried. "For the cellulite to settle?"

Outside in the bright July sun, I jump rope. When my feet are tired of jumping in unison, I skip between them, like running in place, like a buoy bobbing on the water. "Keep jumping," my mother calls down from the deck. I can hear ice clinking in her glass. She is clipping coupons at the white wrought-iron table directly above me. The cat watches from his hiding place, a cool spot under the lawn swing, which floats gently back and forth in the breeze. "Are you sweating?" she shouts. "You need to be sweating. Let's hope you can sweat three croissants out of you by the time your father comes home."

We are far into the summer now, so far that the nights are cool again, and autumn's burnished fingers pinch the horizon at its edges, like wrinkles around an eye. "I like the name Autumn," I remark on the drive to Katy Parker's house. "I think I'd like to name my daughter Autumn—two daughters, Autumn and Amber."

"Yet another reason I'm glad you'll be saving yourself for marriage and your mothering for the years after medical school."

There is no point in correcting her about my future career, but I don't understand what she means about the names. "Do you think they're bad names?"

"Let's just say no grandchildren of mine will be called *Autumn* and *Amber*. Are you living in a fairy tale?"

"No, ma'am." The word glides through my teeth before I can intercept it. This is shoddy vowel work, which my mother is apt to mistake for mockery.

"What did you say?"

"I said, no, *Mom*, not a fairy tale at all."

Katy Parker has locked herself in her bedroom—miraculously, she has a door that locks!—and will not come out, she says, until she is good and ready and her makeup looks just right.

"Honestly," Mrs. Parker sighs, resting her hand on my mother's wrist, "that girl is going to be married—or worse—by the time she's seventeen. . . . Shall I put the kettle on?"

I slide almost unnoticed into their breakfast nook, a sticky turquoise booth that curves with the wall and easily accommodates five.

"What is she up to?" my mother inquires.

"Well, I've told her she's not to see him again, but that senator across the street—*his* son—*Matt*—is apparently quite interested in Katy, even though she's *thirteen* and he's *sixteen*." Each time she whispers a word, Mrs. Parker's voice drops at least one octave and several decibels, making it difficult for me to hear.

"So you'd say she's becoming *boy-crazy* then?" My mother seems cautious, nervous, enunciating her words.

"And how! With brushing her hair a hundred times a day, and the fancy soaps and creams—squandering all her babysitting money—and the *makeup*. . . . Well," Mrs. Parker rubs her large, black glasses on a dish towel. "You must know how that is with Julie."

"Oh, of course. . . ." Her voice trails off.

"Just wait till she fixates all those hormones on a single boy. Just you wait!"

A door slams, and we all turn as Katy makes her entrance. "Katherine Margaret Parker, where do you think you're going—and all dolled up like that?"

"Out," she says in a clipped, confident tone.

"Julie's here, and the two of you should go out together . . . with one stipulation. You are *not* to see that Talmadge boy tonight, understand?"

"Yeah, whatever. Come on, Julie."

"I mean it, young lady." Mrs. Parker follows us into the hall. She is the tallest woman I know, close to six feet, with dark, cropped hair and legs as thin at the top as they are at the bottom. Tonight she wears fitted jeans—dark blue denim with bright gold seams—and a peasant blouse gathered at the neck. In a dress, she would look nearly identical to Popeye's Olive Oyl. At Halloween, she would hardly need a costume.

"I get it, Mom. Julie's with me. We'll go ride bikes or something."

Outside, the evergreens cast their long shadows across the sidewalk, the last traces of sunlight seeping through like honey. This image reminds me I am hungry, that I haven't eaten all day. I follow Katy around the corner of her house, to the part of the yard where rose bushes grow untended, sprawling and toppling over against the warm brick. "These need to be staked," I tell her, "or you could use a trellis and let them climb the length of the wall."

"Forget about that," she whispers. I notice she is wearing her performance makeup, but this time with little sparkles — stars, I think — ornamenting her temples and cheeks. "I need you to wait here and pretend that we've been playing the whole time. Can you do that?"

"What do I do if they come looking for us — for *you*?"

"Then, make something up. I don't know. I'll be back when I can. I just — you wouldn't understand."

"What wouldn't I understand?"

"Matt and I are in love. Our families want to keep us apart, but they won't win. They *can't*."

"It's like the Capulets and the Montagues," I smile.

"The who?"

I shake my head. "It doesn't matter. But I *do* understand."

"Have you ever been, you know, really crazy about someone?"

I think of Mrs. Miller, how she had left our school and gone on, I heard from others, to be a stay-at-home mom. Someone would be lucky to have her, even as a mom. "I guess not," I say. "Not yet."

The rose garden, which is more like a thicket, a great thicket of roses at the apex of bloom, can only hold my interest for a while. By the time it is truly dusk, all the shadows blending together into one dark haze, I turn detective again. "Spying" seems a safer practice than its twin, "voyeurism," the uninvited watching done by those *not* in the gumshoe profession. I slink through the trees. I step warily around the pine cones.

At the Talmadge house, most of the windows are lit, though the curtains are drawn. The inhabitants of the house are oblivious to the happenings in their own sparse garden. Katy Parker leans against the wall. *Why are women always leaning against a wall?* The boy, whom I have never seen up close, is pressed against her. They are kissing vigorously, his hands moving under her shirt.

Perhaps I am a little envious now. I like the idea of being desired, of someone wanting to kiss me that way—with such enthusiasm as he is kissing her. Perhaps being desired is only possible for the skinny girls. I regard my own frame, the way my clothes hang loose over my skin, the way my skin pulls taut over my bones, the compressed feeling inside like two Slinkies in a single box. *Fun for a boy or a girl.*

But there is something else, too. I can't quite put my finger on it, but I know it has to do with what *I* want—with being an agent of desire, not only a recipient. Katy fumbles with his zipper. He reaches down to help her, to draw her hand inside. I look away, partly out of respect for their privacy, and partly. . . . It is a thought I can't finish. *There is no other world but this one*, I murmur, a phrase I have learned somewhere, a phrase that was meant to inspire. I go back to the rose garden and lie down in the grass. I spread the stray petals wide and place them over my eyes.

Today my father will walk me down the aisle. It is not my wedding of course, but my mother snaps picture after picture and daubs at her eyes. "Like a rehearsal," she says. "A rehearsal for your Big Day that won't be so far away now—now that you're thirteen."

The pink lace dress, with its tiers of ruffles and notable absence of straps or sleeves, has become too large since the start of summer. My mother has to fold it in and fasten along the seam with safety pins. No one seems alarmed. In fact, I have received nothing but compliments.

"No sooner did the baby fat come in than she's grown out of it again," our neighbor said, waving over the roof of his truck.

"Now remember what we talked about. This is the last time the judges are going to see you before they make their final decision," my mother instructs. "You need to hold your head up and pull your shoulders back and be sure to make a lasting impression." My father straightens his tie. "As for you, Bill, remember: you're just an accessory. I don't want to see you hamming it up out there."

The lights on the stage burn hotter and brighter than even my dancing days. The auditorium is dark and crowded, pulsing with the body heat and eager breath of hundreds of strangers. "I'm so proud of you," my father whispers. "You look just like an angel."

I almost say, but then I bite my lip—*If I were a son, you'd be proud of me for other things besides my body.* But he means well. My father always means well.

When it is our turn, we step onto the platform. The disembodied announcer's voice booms through the speakers, reading from the biographical statement my mother has written about me. As he reads, we process slowly down the walkway, father and daughter, arm in arm:

"Our next contestant, Julie Marie Wade, hails from Seattle, Washington, where she has distinguished herself as a student of academic excellence. In addition to her high grades and leadership in the classroom, Julie is also a dancer, singer, swimmer, pianist, and downhill skier. She regularly volunteers at the Lutheran Compass Mission and the Hickman House Battered Women's Shelter. When not studying or performing, Julie enjoys reading, cooking, gardening, and playing croquet with her family. She plans to become a pediatrician."

———

Later, I stand alone just offstage, listening as the names of the finalists are called. My mother's pearl and rhinestone necklace weighs on me, heavy against the spears of my collarbones. I long to take it off, to slip into my jeans and sneakers and a ragged t-shirt, the kind my mother only lets me wear at home.

The absence of my name is not a surprise. I cannot even say that I am sorely disappointed. Some of the girls are sobbing now, and somewhere in the vast ballroom, my mother is formulating her explanation for this slight. I stay leaning against the wall, my hip to its groove, watching and waiting. They have narrowed the competition to three girls. They stand in a row, holding each other's hands and grinning. Just beyond the spotlight, a contest affiliate holds the deluxe bouquet of roses, waiting for his cue to release them into the winning girl's arms.

"And the winner of the Miss Pre-Teen America Pageant, who will go on to compete for Miss Teen America, is" . . . a drum roll, a collective intake of breath . . . "Miss Christina Shoemaker!"

She had been chosen. She was the one most heartily admired, or desired, or some combination of both. It might be said that she had preened herself best, of all of us.

Later, my mother would weep, "To think we were going to name you Christina! Think who you might have been if we had!"

Christina Shoemaker wore a dress the color of clear sky with a soft trim of lace and delicate powder blue slippers. She had blond hair and blue eyes and an unblemished face and a body that seemed not to have betrayed her. She could probably dance, too, I imagined, and there was probably a boy somewhere in the wings, waiting for her.

They placed the sparkling tiara on her head and handed her the ribboned assemblage of roses—all garnet-red and long-stemmed with buds just beginning to open. In my mind's eye, I saw her mouth open and fluttering on a boy's mouth, his hands ascending under the ruffles. I heard her apologizing for her perspiration and running to the bathroom to "freshen up." I saw Katy Parker turning a dozen pirouettes without stopping, the dance teacher lauding with applause.

Then, like a keyhole vignette in an old-fashioned movie, the landscapes of memory and imagination narrowed and closed, and everything was eclipsed by the roses.

Four Eyes in a Dark Room

*The alternative is the thrill that comes from leaving the past
behind without rejecting it, transcending outworn or oppressive
forms, or daring to break with normal pleasurable expectations
in order to conceive a new language of desire.*
— Laura Mulvey, "Visual Pleasure and Narrative Cinema"

B efore swimming lessons, you should not eat for two
to three hours. If you have long hair, it should be braided
or otherwise tied back. A cap fitted close to the scalp is prefer-
able, so the chlorine won't turn your hair green. And you will
need a backpack or duffel bag to carry soap, shampoo, a clean
set of clothes, and a warm, wrap-around terry cloth towel. In
addition, waterproof sandals or jelly shoes, which can be worn
in the locker room and out to the edge of the pool. Goggles are
useful if you have trouble opening your eyes underwater.

Most often, a parent will bring you, especially when you
are young. If it is your mother, she may come with you into the
locker room and stretch your swimsuit wide so you can step
your legs one at a time through the spaces, then shimmy the
purple or blue spandex over your shivering skin. After, she will
sit on the bleachers watching you do your backstroke and your
crawlstroke between glances at her *Redbook* magazine.

But if it is your father, because your mother had other plans
that afternoon—your father who is already a little afraid of your
body, though you are still small and flat and smooth as a flushed

torpedo, your white and pink gooseflesh taut as fishing line—
he will leave you at the kiosk where a high school boy wearing
black swim trunks and a hooded sweatshirt that touts his team in
aggrandized letters will ask for your name, check it on a list, and
wave you through to the locker room alone.

Inside you know exactly what you will find—everywhere, the
exposed bodies of women magnified in mirrors: old and young,
toned and slack, slick and shiny or newly dry with a scrubbed
and polished look about them. Even as a child, even before
you have anything to hide, this scene enthralls and terrifies.
You do not feel worthy of your eyes.

  You are struck by how casual they are, how unimpeded by
the perceptions of others. In the showers, women shed swim-
suits like unwanted skins and stand naked, enveloped in steam.
Sometimes they speak to one another of nothing spectacular,
as though it wasn't strange to be uncovered together, sudsing
and rinsing while sharing recipes or reciting the day's news.
They move easily from the showers to the lockers, which gird
this wide, concrete meadow of low benches and hunched bodies like a weald of metal trees.

  There is not an Eve among them, not a fig leaf or frond.
No one bows her head in embarrassment, least of all in shame.
You cannot bring yourself to look, and you cannot bring yourself not to. Without your mother, without the shadow cast by
the thick sheaf of her body, you cannot stand among them,
dressing or undressing, packing or unpacking. You are guilty
already—for a crime you have yet to commit, for a crime that is
not even a crime. Instead, you head down the corridor. Behind
the bright yellow bathroom stall door, its silver latch securely
clasped, your possessions hung on the hook, you slip the loose,
cotton shirt over your shoulders; you slide your legs safely free
from your slacks.

It comes as no surprise, the homophone of "I" and "eye." The
self is comprised of sight, is appraised through the act of seeing.

No wonder you prefer the second person. To be *circumspect* is to attend to the consequences of your behavior, hypothetical or actual, and so this *spect* is girded by two others: *prospect*, a vision of the future, and *retrospect*, a vision of the past.

I will take you back again, in this sidecar called wanting, to something you may have already seen, have already *inspected*. The girl: Mandie Salazar. The place: Southwest Community Center. The event: Janna Blaschke's swimming party in celebration of her eleventh birthday.

First, the girls and boys are divided, changing together in their sexed cocoons, where a presumption of sameness presides. But we are not the same at all! Some of us are tall and gangly, some of us are short and plump, each of us engaged in the metamorphosis from girl to grown-up. It becomes about breasts now: who is budding and who is in full inflorescence. It becomes about blood now: who needs quarters for the wrapped parcels in the gleaming corner machines. It becomes about hair: who is still smooth as a stem and who is beginning to bristle.

Mandie Salazar was my first failed circumspection, which in another language less laden with grief means my first infatuation with a girl my own age. Prudence not possible, wantonness essential, something gave way in me that day by the water. To begin, there was the matter of her softness, which seemed to solicit my touch. There was the matter of her long quilt of hair, which smelled of store-bought nectars and dried thick as a shawl around her shoulders. We had all been wet together, playing and splashing and taking turns on the water slide. I had barely noticed the boys, who were always seeking our attention and then pretending they had no idea why we would stare: their cannonballs so rudimentary, their somersaults amateur and incomplete in a solitary instant of air.

Mandie was the sepia girl in a class photograph who had been subtly turned to color—singled out for this phenomenon called *retouching*—her lips lightly lined with cherry, cheeks blushed with retroactive rouge, hair tinted to reflect its true gold and russet tones. She was the one who stood out, the one I scanned the crowd for when heads bobbed above the surface, when bodies scattered like marbles across the tile shore.

Before this, I think I could have been anyone, perhaps even the one I was intended to be. I could have learned how to look at a boy's body and see, not beauty or lack of beauty, but an invocation of desire. Before this, I might have learned to love a man, not remotely with my mind, but as an honest participant in the physical reflex of longing. I might have hungered after him in my best animal way.

Instead, I climbed the ladder from the deep end, as deep in feet as I was old in years. I liked thinking of the multivalence of numbers. I liked climbing the rungs that in my mind correlated each age with a number, each number with a feeling, each feeling with a person, and then—the rung that trembled like a loose trapeze—a *person* with a *body*.

In Mrs. Blaschke's minivan, as we were crossing the West Seattle Bridge, as the harbor stretched below us toward an unfathomable city of grit and gleam, I felt compelled to kiss her. Despite the witnesses, despite the startled look in her eyes as I leaned forward, my mouth brimming with words I couldn't say—words I had yet to learn—Mandie Salazar was compelled also, for a moment, to receive me. She did not kiss back, but neither did she pull directly away. Before the other girls began to groan, before Mrs. Blaschke regarded me disapprovingly in the rearview mirror, a gentle exchange took place. My pinhole perspective on the world swelled suddenly, luminously, to panorama, wider than the car windows, broader than the bridge or the bay. Nothing was fixed! No one was static! It had been all around me all the time, yet my sight had failed me.

Here's a *spect* I didn't mention before. *Suspect.* Noun, verb, or adjective. Noun, as in *the suspect fled the scene of the crime.* Now change the inflection; emphasize the second syllable instead of the first. Verb, as in *they suspect she was always different from the other girls.* Change the inflection again; put it back as it was before. Adjective, as in *her motives were suspect from the very start.* (Their eyes played tricks; they took things out of context; often, though, they looked for a reason to be wrong.)

Because I did not know the words—*homosexual, lesbian, queer*—I was nothing but self-conscious artillery lacking ammunition. What would it mean to answer to these words? What would it mean to claim them?

After the kiss in the car, Mandie Salazar stopped speaking to me. She made new friends who gawked at me across the playground, who whispered behind me in line at the water fountain, who did not know (any better than I) what they were saying.

In middle school, I made a new start. No one saw me as the girl who kissed Mandie Salazar. I was defined less by a specific deviation and more by a general description: the girl who was strange and awkward with bad acne and bulbous glasses, who played chess at recess and wore ridiculous dresses and always made impeccable grades. I was known simply, and paradoxically, as someone who was not known.

But at home, close scrutiny kept me perennially suspect. Reticence meant hoarding secrets; sociability, covering my tracks. And this concept of *respect*, which seemed to mean "to look again, to reconsider"—to see more fully, and as a consequence, to treat well—was extended to me, an empty promise, an egg whose yolk had been siphoned out of its shell.

"You've always been weird," my mother complained. "Other girls *want* to wear lipstick. They *want* to go to the mall. What is it? What's the matter with you?"

But so much mattered it was impossible to say! I waited day after day in passive desperation for my life to have its way with me—to force a change. This change came first and most notably in the form of an invitation. My Aunt Linda on my father's side, who also fell under my mother's wide-sweeping suspicion, had decided to begin swimming again. She felt old and out of shape, and her body all but demanded a return to this low-impact, vigorous exercise.

"I already stay at your grandma's house on Wednesday nights as it is, and now there's an Adult Swim offered on Wednesday nights, and my friend Dale is going, and I would love it if you wanted to come along." She was the only person in our family with green eyes. When she looked at me, I was mesmerized.

We arrived at the Southwest Community Center in my aunt's aging car, a blond Mustang rusted around the rims and pocked in places by the inevitable dents and scrapes of many years' wear. Linda also had been at one time so effortless in beauty: the smooth white skin, the soft blond hair, best Nordstrom-brand clothes shrouding her slim arrow of a torso. As I sat on the cracked, caramel upholstery of the broken back seat, I saw how my aunt looked different now from her classic photographs: sweat pants, a puffy-painted t-shirt from a local beach shop, a visor pulled low to hide her graying bangs.

Dale waited for us outside the building, her taut, tan body neatly packaged in pleated shorts and a towel fastened across her shoulders with a hair clip. Beneath it, a plain lady swimsuit flattened her breasts in a strange, unflattering way. She ate corn chips from a plastic bag and waved and shouted and called my aunt "Lindy" as we approached.

"I got worried you had chickened out!" she called, darting toward us with arms outstretched. I thought how her small frame could barely contain the gist of her, like a jack-in-the-box wound to bursting or a can of party snakes destined to explode.

"This must be your niece. Wow, look at you!" she smiled.

"Please don't." Yet it was difficult at the same time to stay bashful in her presence. I wanted to tell her things. I wanted to see what she saw.

"Right—so James—that's my husband, bless his heart— we call him *sweet baby James* after the James Taylor song—

do you know it?"—I didn't, but I nodded just the same, not wanting her to have to stop and explain—"James *loves* the idea of me making this Wednesday night swim a regular thing because he wants to watch some terrible show on television and have the remote all to himself. He says to me, 'And when you're done swimming, you might as well go out for a hot fudge sundae or something,' and I told him, 'Honey, you're missing the whole point,' but then I thought, Well, what the hell. Maybe we *should* go out for a hot fudge sundae after. What do you say?"

Inside the locker room, I felt familiar tensions resurface. All around us: those confident women, those keen, prepubescent girls. I was coming into my body then, an incomplete Etch A Sketch of a woman with all the worst parts drawn in first. Dale laid down her cloth purse—burgundy, a long shoulder strap adorned with tiny violets. It gaped with admirable, grown-up things: an apple, a wire brush, a row of pink-pack deodorant tampons, Pert Plus 2-in-1 conditioning shampoo. She stood out in the center of the room, unzipping her shorts, unclasping her towel, pulling a tight, squeaky cap over short, tousled, salt-and-pepper gray hair.

But my aunt, who was approaching fifty then, who was tall and round-shouldered and unsure of herself, who brought a swimsuit with a black ruffled skirt and a long robe to wear over it, receded immediately to the bathroom. Dale nudged me with a pitying look, murmured only, "I thought she'd be over that by now."

I stood trembling. I didn't want anyone to see my body. I feared indifference as much as I feared reproach. What if no one could find me beautiful? I had just read about Gregor Samsa. Every morning I wondered if I would wake as a bug, if the most repulsive part of me had stopped being dormant, had shifted, was about to hatch. But even more than this fear, I wanted Dale to like me, to think me easygoing and energetic, to distinguish me from my emotionally frayed, underconfident aunt. I bent down to unlace my shoes. I held everything still on the inside. In this way, I learned exposure can be another way to hide.

To look is not always to see. That is one difficulty. There are others. Boys and girls are taught to look differently, first in how they *appear*, and second, in how they *regard*. To look is both passive and active, a way of being and an intense, concentrated mode of observation.

The girls I knew were learning how to be looked at, to become mannequin-like in the mirror-windows. My father had said more than once, "You need to learn how to take a compliment." He meant, *You need to learn how to comply.* Boys were looking all the time, and we were expected to receive their looks gratefully, modestly. How vain it would be to revel overtly! Yet how cruel to imply we cared nothing at all for their eyes! Suddenly, I seemed a huge moth pinned at my wing-tips by scrutiny. The red velvet cushion of the display case had been meticulously laid out for me. This was not punishment. The glass came down quietly, without malice.

The summer I turned fifteen, we spent a long day on Maury Island. We traveled by ferry. I wore my swimsuit under my clothes. I was conscious of having become an island myself, separated from the mainland by some considerable distance. By certain accounts, I was impossible to reach.

Standing on the beach, I felt the reassuring insulation of sunlight, the growing afternoon heat. Erin and Jennifer, my classmates, lingered up on the hill where someone's father was grilling. They had plastic chairs and suntan oil and Scrabble. No one would miss me if I stretched out by this log, stripped down to bare legs and brown shoulders.

I opened my eyes to find someone blocking my sun, a tall shadow with sharp, pronounced ribs. "Are you Erin's friend?" he asked.

"Our parents are friends," I replied.

"Oh—Julie, right?"

I shifted, making a small shield from the light with my hand. "Do I know you?"

"Rob," he said. "I'm Erin's cousin. We haven't met before."

He sat down next to me, and I was aware that his eyes had been combing my body, like a gull scouring a landscape for unopened shells. It was predatory in some way, but he was not unkind. Sixteen, seventeen at most, he was looking for what he was supposed to find. "They wanted me to tell you the burgers are done. They have hot dogs too, and veggie dogs— in case you're a vegetarian."

"I'm not," I said, leaning back on the log with no intention of moving.

"Are you hungry?"

"Not really."

He seemed stumped and wanting to please me, perplexed that he didn't know how. "Back at the house, we've got some licorice and fortune cookies. Maybe later you'd like to have some?"

"Ok. Maybe." I didn't want to commit to anything. I couldn't bring myself to make it easy for him.

"We're also going swimming in a little while, and my uncle's planning to take the speedboat out, if you want to ride."

"Sure," I said. "In a little while."

After he had gone, I thought how I had strangely enjoyed the attention. We were all thespians, and this mild flirtation had seemed an oddly pleasing performance. *Was it possible for once I was cast as lead?* After all, I had been taking Accutane. My skin was clear, my legs cleanly shaven. I stood taller and leaner, curving out and cinching in at predictable intervals, my body leading me toward some new imperative.

I returned to the house that day, snug in my small power. In the basement, which was only beanbag chairs strewn across a red-and-gold shag carpet, we ate licorice and fortune cookies from an enormous wood bowl. Rob patted his lap, and I sank down into it, with a feeling like relief or surrender. Jennifer looked on, disapproving. I knew she was religious. Maybe she thought we were moving too fast. Maybe she was jealous. All I knew was, unaccustomed to such attention, I needed to follow it through.

Rob cannon-balled from the deck of the speedboat, then beckoned for me to join him. Shivering already, I took the plunge as a summons to experiment. He was my carnation in a cup of colored water. He was my contraption designed to measure heat and pressure, my mouse maze and papier-mâché piñata.

"I want to kiss you," he said. I liked his candor.

"But you can't. Someone on the boat or the shore might see."

We were treading in place, our legs working hard, our hands lightly sculling.

"I want to touch you," he said. I wished I could be frank about desire.

"So what's stopping you?"

His hand moved over my breast. We sunk lower until only our heads were visible, our chins resting on the water. He pulled my swimsuit down and caressed me. It wasn't fair to him really. I was already numb before he began, the Sound so cold, even in August.

"You can touch me, too," he said. I tried. I laid both hands against his chest. "Lower," he urged.

The speedboat was circling back now, but we were still clandestine, still holding fast. We could have gone to the room with the beanbag chairs and closed the curtains. We could have sneaked away to one of the inlets in the deep, wet sand. For so long, I had abandoned my body. Perhaps this boy could redeem me, could reach for the switch on the wall of awful indifference and complete the pun after all—could *turn me on*.

Even my mother had remarked, earlier that same day: "Joe

Boden was staring at you out the kitchen window, and you couldn't even offer him a smile?"

Later on, my back pressed to the red brick wall, the pleasant sun on my salt-laced skin, I let him kiss me some and told him I'd send letters. I wrote one:

> *Dear Rob,*
> *We're at the beach in Oregon. More sand and fewer*
> *stones down here. This postcard shows the end of the*
> *Lewis and Clark Trail, two men who found what they*
> *were looking for. Let's hope we're as lucky.*

The last time I went to Adult Swim with Aunt Linda and Dale was during my final days of high school. This event had become more of a social hour than a commitment to rigorous exercise. We didn't mind. We took our kickboards and floated out in one of the slow lanes, flutter- and frog-kicking the length of the pool, talking and laughing all the while.

I didn't want to lose my easy rapport with these women. They had met years before when Linda pledged Dale's sorority in college. This made them sisters of a kind, who bunked together on huge sleeping porches and curled each other's hair for ritual fraternity functions.

"So what sororities are you interested in?" Dale asked as we lollygagged on the smooth Jacuzzi ledge.

I took a deep breath. "None, actually. I'm not going to pledge."

"You're not serious! Linda, do you hear this?" My aunt returned to us, swaddled in terrycloth, her hair twisted up in a towel.

"I've tried to change her mind, but she's a grown girl. In the end, only she can decide."

"But it was so important, the relationships we formed with other women—look at Linda and me! We're still friends all these years later." Dale laid her soft, veiny hand on my shoulder. "Linda was my maid of honor!"

"Well, I'm not really looking to assemble a wedding party," I replied.

"No, of course not, but it happens. You meet the women who will be there for you through thick and thin—marriages, divorces, *God forbid*, the birth of your children—" Neither Dale nor my aunt had borne any children, but our conversation never bent that way.

I didn't know how to say I feared sororities even more than locker rooms, how they seemed to me like *living* inside a locker room: so much changing together, and whispered gossip, and sharing a close space without enough curtains or robes. When they kissed each other, it was tender, familial. If deeply, it was "practicing" for men. I didn't want to kiss women under false pretenses, and by then I knew Mandie Salazar wasn't a fluke. She foreshadowed a truth I buried in myself like treasure.

"Seen any good movies lately?" I inquired, anxious to move the conversation along.

"As a matter of fact, you won't believe what was on the other night!" Dale's dark brows lifted. "Linda, do you remember when we first saw *Psycho*—how terrified I was?"

My aunt slipped her feet into the fizzy water, sighed. "Dale didn't sleep for weeks. She was a basket case."

"That shower scene! Oh my good lord! I thought Norman Bates was coming for *me*!"

"So what's the verdict . . . all these years later?"

"Well, it surprised me," Dale replied, sliding her lower torso beneath the bubbling surface. "It surprised me because it was *just as terrifying* as I remembered! I don't know how Alfred Hitchcock ever washed himself again!"

"Maybe he took baths," I suggested.

"That's such a British thing to do—come over to America, make your masterpiece, give us all insomnia, and head back home to your bath salts and bubbles!" Dale was strutting around in the water like a wet chicken, gesturing wildly between grateful pauses with half-closed eyes. "Oh, this feels spectacular! Get in, both of you, get in!"

Aunt Linda and I submerged ourselves in tandem, letting the jets massage our necks and spines. I cherished our easy camaraderie, the way we could be together, speaking or silent, supported by a mutual affirmation. I knew for my aunt and Dale, their sorority had promised them exactly that. But they were confirmed heterosexuals; they could expect to find a world of women who would receive them, affirm them. I feared already that women would not trust me if they knew my secret, that I would seem a spy peering at them through traitorous eyes.

Just then, a tall, slender man wearing only a lavender Speedo appeared on the ledge. "Do you ladies mind if I join you?" he asked. It was an intention framed as a question. What could we say?

"Well, it's a bit crowded," Dale remarked. "Enter at your own risk."

Mistaking her disdain for flirtation, the man—hairy, pasty-skinned, mid-forties—eagerly descended. "I'm quite a risk-taker," he said. "Don't mind if I do."

And there we were, three women sharing one bench, a man seated opposite us, taking up space, blithely staring. I felt my stomach turn, not at the fact of him who had a right to exist and a right to choose to take his hot tub at precisely that moment—a right, in fact, to be confident and undeterred in the presence of women who did not want him there—but imagining myself in college, in *life*, as a version of this intrusive, undesirable man.

We clammed up the moment he arrived. I feared then that the real purpose of women's togetherness was formed in resistance to men, based upon and necessitated by a certain sexual tension. My preference for women's company, if exposed, presented an unforgivable nakedness.

The man in the lavender Speedo tried his best to make small talk. At times, I felt sorry for him, pruny and overzealous, desperate for some sign of success. He was wishing for us to stay, we were longing for him to go, a standoff of the sexes staged against this backdrop of froth and bubbles. At last, he proposed, "Sauna anyone?" Dale and Linda avidly declined, and I allowed their response to speak for me. "What about you?"

"Me?"

"Yes, *you*—pretty girl in the middle. Care to join me?"

I looked at him. For the first time, I think I really met his eyes. And I saw in his eager, defenseless face something I recognized, with which I empathized but which I also despised. It was a complicated feeling, the sense that he was already, or would become, the portrait of my competition.

When I was fourteen, I watched *Psycho* for the first time with my father. He said, "You know the saddest thing is that Anthony Perkins was gay and died of AIDS."

"That *is* sad," I replied.

I don't know if he heard himself speaking, if he meant anything by it: "Yes, and his death of AIDS was sad, too."

When I was twenty-three, I watched the *Psycho* remake for the first time with my lover. She said, "You know, Anne Heche used to be gay until she went crazy."

This time I could smile. This time I could quip: "It's crazy *not* to be gay."

Everyone watched Marion Crane in the shower. Most of us knew about the chocolate syrup that substitutes for blood. Some of us knew that Janet Leigh had trouble showering thereafter; she explained about this on a talk show—how she had to leave the door open, even as water flooded the floor. How does this image, her body dismembered into montage to avoid showing everything, to prevent nudity from becoming *lewd*, shape our collective unconscious? Who are we in this story? Victims, villains, voyeurs? (All three?) How culpable are we for the way this story ends?

Once, I dreamed I had been blindfolded at a party where everyone was playing Pin the Tail on the Donkey. For my turn, the game became a strange kind of Spin the Bottle. If I kissed the right person, I would be able to see again. Alone in the dark, I wandered for what seemed hours, frightened as the crowd dispersed and my mouth grew desperately parched. When I met a man on the forest path, I begged him to kiss me—to set me free. Instead, he reached up and untied the blindfold. "I think you need glasses," he said.

In my waking life, I *had* glasses. I had worn them since I was five but stopped after high school. It was neither a sudden nor a symbolic change. My vision had not improved; my perspective had not enlarged. I simply wanted to begin watching the world as it appeared to me, the world that I was able to see.

But the dream reminded me that I was not so carefree. It hearkened back to freshman philosophy when we studied George Berkeley's subjective idealism, summed up in the phrase "esse est percipi"—*to be is to be perceived*. What this meant to me, glasses or no, was that we all saw the world through four eyes, the two with which we looked out, and the two with which we looked in. Introspection was not merely the act of observing yourself; it was the act of seeing yourself *being seen*. How did you *look* to others? How did you *seem*?

What I didn't want was to seem creepy somehow. I knew what it meant to be ogled by men, whether the gaze contained an admiring or menacing core. Women were supposed to want them to look. I didn't. I had tried to care, but I couldn't. Yet even the women who yearned for this visual caress wanted, in more cases than not, to be seen fully—not the peephole view but the panorama.

My first-year, random-assignment roommate was a tall, lithe swimmer named Rebecca Farrell. Before I ever laid eyes on her, I fell in love with her smooth, well-syllabled name. It was a name that seemed to give way to her person, warm and open, possessed of an accessible beauty, an unintimidating grace.

"Good to meet you, Julie," she grinned, shaking my hand heartily, so that my fingers pressed against her moonstone ring.

"You too, Rebecca," I smiled.

"Oh, you can call me Becky, by the way."

At once, the woman before me bifurcates into Becky, the imminent friend, and Rebecca, the imagined lover. I allow her to occupy two places in my mind—the real body on the captain's bed, only an arm's length away, and the unraveling thread of my daily memory of her, stretched across a cat's cradle of incommunicable desire.

Becky touches me often and fondly; we talk with ease. Rebecca does not know I exist, does not listen for my fretful breath as I lay sleepless in our mutual dark.

It is not long before the men come. They are coming for her, for her gentle certainty, her blond and cordial beauty. "Is your roommate here?" they inquire. They look past me through the parted door. "Becky, I'm looking for Becky."

And I admire their gusto and their nerve at least as much as I resent their intrusion. They never call first. They take their chances. They want, more than anything, to see her face to face.

"She's swimming," I say, whether it is true at the moment or not. "I couldn't say when she'll be back. Would you like me to tell her you stopped by?"

Ari is the most persistent. He is looking for a girlfriend, not merely a good time. He has never gone longer than three months without one, he confides, which is important. A man needs a woman beside him, especially a minister, which is what Ari aspires to be. He is tall, gaunt, acned, a late adolescent version of Ichabod Crane. Becky, it seems, is his Katrina.

"Do you mind if I wait?" he asks, another intention disguised as an inquiry.

"That's fine," I say, gesturing toward the beanbag chairs we have arranged. "Make yourself comfortable."

Ari is quiet, but I am aware of his pale blue eyes roving the room, studying our photographs and wall-hangings for clues. Hunched over my desk, I try to concentrate on the page until his eyes bore holes in my back, drilling for answers. Finally, I give up and turn around.

"So, are you and Becky in biology together?" I probe.

"No—not that I don't love biology. I do. But I've decided to become an English major."

"Really?"

"What's your major?" he inquires, half-interested, half-passing time.

"Psychology—though I'm thinking about an English major, too."

We study each other between awkward glances toward the door that does not open. Ari makes practiced conversation about his string of former girlfriends, all of whom he hopes will join his wedding party someday. "It's a misperception I think that when people break up, they have to stop being friends; they have to stop seeing each other all together. Who made that rule? Just because two people aren't destined to become spouses doesn't mean they can't remain close."

"Do you actually think people are destined to become spouses?"

His brows tightly knit, perplexed: "As opposed to what?"

"Anything, I guess."

"I have these friends who got married over the summer, and they had never kissed each other until they took their vows in a church with all their friends and family watching."

A laugh escapes my lips. "Is there something funny?"

"Well, I mean, that sounds kind of crazy to me. These people dated each other and never kissed, got engaged to each other without any kind of physical contact?"

Growing defensive now, shifting on the sunken chairs:

"They held hands. They hugged each other. They just saved their first kiss for that perfect moment at the altar."

I glance at the clock and let my eyes linger. I don't have anywhere to be, anything to do, but he doesn't know that. After a few moments, Ari stands up and mumbles something about leaving Becky a note on the white board. "That sounds like a fine idea," I patronize.

"By the way—" poking his head back through the door, his long neck like a turtle's craning out of its shell—"I'm not saying that *I* could wait until marriage for a kiss. It's a nice idea, but to my mind, quite impractical."

At night, late into the night, Becky's lamp on, reading. I listen to the rustle of her pages, remind myself to breathe. Roll over, close my eyes, recall each word of our most recent conversation.

"I'm surprised, with all the reading you do, that you don't wear glasses," she remarks.

"I used to. Not so much anymore."

"I like them, you know. Not so much for seeing—I mean, that's what contacts are for—but as an accessory, a fine pair of spectacles—maybe oval-shaped with tortoise-shell frames— seems more memorable than . . . I don't know . . . more striking than a *watch* at least."

"So, these *spectacles* . . . they're like . . . bracelets . . . for your face?"

"Something like that, yeah." And then we both burst into sleepy, puerile laughter.

In the locker room again, that recurring dream—the kind that overtakes me, holds me hostage to its whims. I have come with Becky, at her request, for an afternoon lap swim at the university pool. I do my best not to notice her body, not to let her notice me working so hard not to notice. I am frightened by the spectacle love threatens to create, the spectacle love threatens to become.

"I'm just not attracted to him," she says. "I'll talk to any-body—you know that—but I don't want to give him the wrong idea."

I don't say much. I rummage through my bag in search of goggles.

"Do you think I need to be more frank with him?"

"Maybe. It's obvious he likes you, and you wouldn't want to lead him on."

"True. . . . And he's been hinting about Homecoming, and that's just the last thing I need." She struggles with her necklace, then lifts her thick canopy of hair: "Julie, would you mind?"

My fingers tremble as I take the clasp. There are tiny white hairs at the nape of her neck, a row of them, standing on end.

"You know the other thing about Ari"—turning her head to the side, attempting to meet my eyes—"is that he doesn't seem much like the girlfriend kind."

Releasing her locket then, passing it over her shoulder and dropping it into her hand. "No? What does he seem like?"

"*Gay*." She whispers the word, as though it is not worthy of full volume.

"How can you tell?" I ask, avoiding her eyes, wrapping my body tightly in a towel.

"Just a feeling I have, the feeling that he's trying too hard."

"Maybe he just likes you," I offer.

"No, it's not the same as with other boys. He's compensating for something. Maybe he doesn't even realize."

I follow Becky down the concrete corridor, through the steam of the showers, toward the stale heat and chlorine stench of the pool. Becky knows things. She can read people. It is only a matter of time before she peers into my queer, quivering heart and glimpses these treasons: the practiced casualness, the tensing up when she touches me, all my self-censorship and nervous twitches.

There is only one thing to do—pretend to like Ari. We are both desperate. Would he take the bait? Oh please, Ari, pretend to like *me!*

There is a symmetry to our language I have always admired, a symmetry that allows me to lean on the windowsill of a certain word and gaze across the courtyard to its converse. If my worst fear was to create a *spectacle*, an unwelcome reason for others to inspect me closely, or for me to inspect myself, then it seemed only logical that the alleviation of this fear would result when attention was taken away.

In his opening remarks at the International Camouflage Conference, which took place at the University of Northern Iowa in April 2006, poet Marvin Bell offered the following observation:

> it occurred to me that, like anything camouflaged, poetry doesn't easily reveal itself. At first glance, it looks and sounds like the utilitarian language we use every day, but it isn't. It can be the lie that tells the truth. It can follow an indirect path that reveals more than a straight line would. If its subject matter is controversial, it can dress so as not to be easily recognized for what it is. In other words, to see it, one sometimes has to take a second look. And, indeed, one can be looking directly at it and not see it until it moves.

Camouflage! Ari's purpose in my life was to disguise me, to help me to appear as I was not. I too yearned for a "utilitarian language," one comprised of boyfriends and girlfriends, hand-holding and tongue-kissing, a public courtship superimposed upon a private scrutiny. People would see us together without noticing. Or their noticing of us would impede insight into the real story of our lives. But unlike "the lie that tells the truth," this way of living—being seen with someone to avoid being seen alone, to avoid, above all, a certain milieu of *speculation* — I performed the converse daily: a truth that gradually revealed a lie.

It didn't last long, my romance with Ari. He was a Christian, so we couldn't go *far*, and I was skeptical still, so we couldn't go *deep*. Mostly, we skimmed the surface.

For a few months, we each held an umbrella over the other's head, the bright yellow umbrella of courtesy and couplehood to deflect a relentless and sometimes perilous rain. As actors, we never missed our marks, our cues. We stepped on the little glow-tape squares and projected loudly enough so every member of the audience could hear. On New Year's, we took Becky, who had become our pretty blond beard — our mutual bond to attractiveness and normalcy — out with us to see a movie.

The cinema is the most perfect counterpoint to the locker room. The exhibitionists are all on screen; no one notices the composition of the observers. I could sit in that dark for hours. I could kiss anyone, let anyone kiss me. Never in my life have I felt such perfect anonymity, such freedom to be no one — and yet, simultaneously, the freedom to be everyone I see.

Like the locker room, the screen is nothing if not relentless montage, body after body passing like shadows as if through the projectionist's dreams. Unlike the locker room, we are all forward-facing, hearts racing and eyes following a single trajectory.

As I once wrote in my journal, "In the dark, it doesn't matter who you love."

Picture us there: The Lewis and Clark Theater, with its grand façade, its red brocade curtains drawn dramatically back in time with the entr'acte; Becky to my right, Ari to my left, the screen-light waxing and waning.

No one mentioned resolutions, though undoubtedly we all had made them. This word also suggests a way of seeing, a clarity of focus that is comparable to a clarity of purpose. We wipe clean the screens of our minds, removing smudges. We tuck our hand-kerchiefs back in our pockets, or perhaps arrange them askew beneath the lapel, hoping an intrepid viewer will notice.

This film is the story of three unlikely friends. On the surface, it is a love story between Melvin the writer and Carol the wait-ress. But it is also a love story between Carol the waitress and Simon the artist and between Simon the artist and Melvin the writer. No one has sex and the kisses are loaded with meaning, so we understand that this movie is not about cheap thrills, though we would gladly take them if offered. It is also, in part, a love story between Carol the waitress and every member of the audience. Like Becky, she is tall, lithe, and blond. She has a sharp wit and a sincere generosity. We are meant to love her, to look at her and to love her, which is not hard.

Then, there is Simon, who is gay. I have only seen movies where gay people are punished, and this one is no exception, at least at first. Simon is beaten and robbed, attacked in his own home, perhaps expected to die. But before all that, before the narrative plunges and later resolves, he has a conversation with a young man complicit in his demise: "You ever watch someone who doesn't know you're watching?" I am nodding in my mind. At the movies, every utterance and every gesture is meant for me. "And you see this flash come over them and you know immediately that it has nothing to do with anything external. . . ."

Ari is holding my hand. Becky is wearing her glasses. I covet the hands folded in her lap, hands I cannot take in mine without arousing suspicion.

On the screen, Simon's eyes are bright and blue, glossy with tears. It is his big Hollywood moment, and the skeptic in me has temporarily retired. "If you look at someone long enough, you discover their humanity," he says.

I will go home. I will think about the movie. Perhaps, in my future life, I will have reason enough to walk in the rain without an umbrella, the way Carol the waitress does—*purposefully*—on her way to Melvin's apartment. Because love is so strange, and foreign to me as the streets of New York City, yet familiar too, as the flush of embarrassment when she discovers her shirt is soaked through, her nipples pert and visible beneath the cotton.

I will go home. I will think about the movie. I will leave Ari on the doorstep and Becky asleep in her bed. I will think again of the best *spect* there is—the *prospect*. In the dark, it doesn't matter who I love.

Triptych of My Aunt Linda, Poet in Her Own Right, Frightened of Bicycles

First Panel

In the summer of 1953, her scarlet fever. A brick house in a new suburb in Washington State, where she would sleep for days while her brother—the older, the healthy, the wiser—played. He brought his friends sometimes, and they stood outside her window and tossed tiny stones, rousing her from the bed where she lay sweating, swaddled in mummy clothes, and sang songs about spiders scaling drain pipes and Mary's albino lamb.

But there was the boy who came back again—Ned or Tom or some other monosyllabled name. He was "always in need of a good spanking," the neighbors said, "full of the dickens," her mother said, though she never saw him creeping around the side of the house to the woodshed where a bright red bicycle was stored. It had handlebars like rams' horns and a smooth white seat cushioned and faintly ribbed—to prevent her skinny hind from slipping off—and it was waiting there for Linda to get well so she could ride.

This boy, whom we shall call Dickens, dinged the little

silver bell and gazed up at the window until an anemic angel appeared, so blond and white she might have been mistaken for a half-poached egg. Then he smiled, a grin laced with malice and flirtation (how she would confuse them over the length of her riddled life!), and the threat that this bicycle, *her* bicycle, which she was not yet able to ride, had never yet ridden— which was purchased for her by her traveling salesman father who could not be there always, though he tried—would be taken away, would be *confiscated*. Her skin flamed, and her nostrils flared, and she stamped her feet and attempted to scream—but he would put the bicycle back before anyone saw him, and her voice would come only a trickle, like sink-drip or the slush at the end of a stream.

Second Panel

At sixteen, she is plagued with dreams. By day, they tell the story of some boy looking, or of wanting him to look, wishing he would say *something* as he passed her in the hall. A dream of white lace, of leisure. A dream of children, who appear without pain and linger at her feet: astute, devoted. A clean, white apron. Being taken out, shown off, sought for advice and admired for style. "Look at what Linda is wearing!" the other women would gasp in awe—*awe*, with a garnish of envy, like the cherry in a Tom Collins or the tonic in a shot of gin. Not that she knows quite about these things, but she imagines. She watches, and she imagines, and what she doesn't know, she invents, the way women before her, from far less, spun clothes and baked bread from meager material.

Night is another story. She drinks warm milk and sinks into a feather bed, where she is swallowed alive, and the first of the night terrors begin. A man comes to her in the dream and says, "You're gonna push this up the stairs." She says, "What?" And he says, "*this*," and there's her bicycle again, only the red has faded and the front wheel has grown smaller and the back wheel has grown larger, so it's a circus bike now, fit for a clown, a clown on a tightrope perhaps. Still, the man insists, prodding her with his foot, "Push this. Up there." She's in the Capitol building now, where they went once on a field trip and where she remembers being scared by the tall staircase with no handrail that kept winding higher and higher into the unseen sky. *"Push! There!"* The commands turn short, brusque, and he puts his hands on her—she remembers the foul talc of his stained white gloves—and moves her forcibly toward the first step. Should she press the bicycle ahead or drag it behind? *"Now!"*

His bark rises to the rounded dome and ricochets along the walls and back again, a multi-toned bellow. The sweat streams down her back, flooding her hands so she can barely grasp what she is hauling, the great beast of vinyl and wire with its improbable, poorly proportioned wheels.

"And I just knew," she says, taking a sip of sweet blackberry wine and looking just as I recall her across the kitchen table—sheepish and forlorn—"that nothing I did would ever matter."

I think of her, sixteen and struggling, her neck turned to poultice, her perspiring palms, the bicycle chipped to pink and skittering over the edge like a piece of apocalypse, or a very large peppermint candy.

Third Panel

Now the greeting cards are fraught with fragmented imperatives—*Do something every day that scares you.* In her forties, she buys a mountain bike, spends more than she should, cautiously crests the smooth dirt trails of Marymoor Park. This is where the bicyclists go. They have hand signals and travel in packs. How she wishes she could join them, renounce this isolated imposter braking before the downhill even begins.

Elsewhere, in her grounded life, she meets a man who loves bicycles. He travels fearlessly without helmet or gloves. His hands are rough, his expression one of bemused assurance. *Could he love her?* This is not the question she asks, but the question she ponders. They spread picnic blankets and share pâté. Together, they assess the virtues of eight-dollar wine, the nostalgia for woven baskets. Little girls ride by with training wheels, streamers gleaming from their handlebars. Banana seats and bells. She regrets their first meeting, years before, when she rebuffed him and his bumbling advance. Before he was divorced with teenaged children. Before she left her childbearing years behind. It seemed her whole life she had been living in an After.

One weekend she leaves town. Friends have invited her to visit in the Islands. She tells him good-bye. He will call her Sunday night, meet her at the ferry docks and walk her home. "What's happening with you and Chuck?" her friends inquire. She cannot answer. To speak of him would spoil things. Is this romance, camaraderie? The same questions surface again—childish questions she wants to condemn but can't quite ignore—*Are they friends, or more than friends?*

When Chuck dies, he flies over the handlebars of the sleek, well-polished machine. She tries to imagine him a phoenix, but the picture will not hold, will not set. The way it always is—*a freak accident*—a heart attack that no one saw coming. Such a healthy man, they said. Strong limbs, low cholesterol. Was it too much cheap wine? He once joked that "abstinence could kill a man." Had *she* done this to him? Might *she* be the culprit after all?

Her bicycle dangles upside down in her mother's woodshed, put up for good. When she closes this door, she will also cover the windows. She doesn't fret. Instead, a new thought polishes her tenderness until a glossy coat of apathy appears. Just as the map of the flat world bends back on itself and becomes round . . . the wolf is always inside the sheep, she observes, even as the ewe quivers, gnaws the new grass, watches timidly over her shoulder.

Meditation 29

What is the late November doing
With the disturbance of the spring . . .
Late roses filled with early snow?

—T. S. Eliot, "East Coker"

Spring 2008.

Ohio spring comes slowly, if at all. Winter before summer, like one foot in front of the other. No one believes the trees will blossom. Blue-tinged, woolly clouds descend, trifle with new fruits in the orchard. Crocuses tremble; tulips bow down. Overnight, the white eraser comes to wipe them out. *Tabula rasa*, the skies repeat. *Tabula rasa.*

I am here for this snowfall. I have been here for others. We are *wintering* in a land far colder than the one we came from. Is this counterintuitive? "We should have moved to Florida," Angie says. "Even Texas is starting to sound good." In the hallway: buttoning our coats, slipping mittens over twitching fingers. How can I explain my growing fondness for the cold, the urgent freshness? How can I tell her, in this barren place, the snow provides our only replenishment, emboldening the poet's first dictum, *MAKE IT NEW?*

On the concrete stairs, a smooth layer of ice has formed. The snow conceals it. We step down, one foot in front of the other. At the landing, Angie falls forward on her knees—graceful and slow, the posture of sudden prayer. I am walking behind her, stride for stride. As I slide off the stair, both feet in the air, flexing then pointing (an ancient muscle-memory of ballet . . .), my body stretches long. In the perfect caesura between two states of being—rising and falling, trusting and doubting—I linger here in unintended levitation. My palms are open; I want all yet grasp for nothing. (How Miss Erika's back, its topos of black moles and taut sinew, bent and turned before me at the barre. . . .)

Then, the blood. *It's like a Pollock painting*, I think. I thought. Did I say the words aloud? Angie was peering down at me. I felt the heat rushing out of my head. Long hallways gushing with blood. *The Shining*. Ligeti's rapturous score. *Is this my life flashing in front of my eyes?* I think. I thought. *The moon on the breast of the new-fallen snow gave the luster of mid-day to objects below.* It was true! All around me, despite the night, shone a luster of midday. But where was the moon? I had recited that poem every Christmas of my childhood, yet somehow never heard the words before, never listened to the sound of my own voice speaking. "You have to sit up," Angie insisted. My body so cold, and still the heat rushing out of my head. *Snow White and Rose Red*. The perfect contrast. A Stephen King story? A spinning wheel? Someone pricked her finger, and it bled. Wasn't it Eliot who said, *In my beginning is my end?*

Cleda, from the boarding school, drives us to the hospital—three miles in blizzard conditions, but she has a truck with studded tires. Cleda has lived in this town her whole life, birthed five babies at this hospital, "seen worse spills than this one," gesturing abstractly toward the gash in my head. I notice that snow falls the way they say a hush falls; I've only heard it pronounced in the past tense before—*a hush had fallen*. Both of these imply a mythic sort of silence. Now the heater hums softly, and in the warm dark, Angie takes my hand.

"You know that man, Phineas Gage?" I whisper. "I'll never

forget him. He came back a different person after damage to his brain."

"You're not damaged," she smiles. "Just woozy."

"But who would I be?" I wonder. *If I could start fresh. If I could turn new.*

She squeezes my palm. "Maybe someone who doesn't talk so much."

Squinting in the sour light of the Barnesville emergency room, I let the doctor examine me—my head, my eyes. "You're a lucky young lady," he says. "A quarter-inch in any direction, and they'd have had to wheel you in on a stretcher."

"I didn't see stars," I tell him. *But where was the moon?* "I never lost consciousness."

"Good girl"—tapping my knee with his tiny hammer.

"I was afraid—I know it sounds silly—that all my words were going to leak out of my head." Then, suddenly self-conscious: "I'm a teacher, so I'd be instantly unemployed, to say nothing of—" The doctor is busy now, parting my hair, daubing my wound with gentle, almost parental care. "You know, I've heard of *aphasia* before. I always remember words I like the sound of. But the concept terrifies me. I *need* my words, and not just a few of them either. I'm greedy. I like to keep more than my share." (An image of my mother caulking tile, stacking newspapers wall-to-wall inside her "slow-draining" shower.) He opens the bandage, shakes out the butterfly wings.

"The head is extremely *vascular*—there's a word for you. That's doctor-talk for 'bleeds a lot,' which is why injuries here—" his hand cupped to my skull like a Sunday blessing— "often seem worse than they actually are. I want you to go home, take this very strong Tylenol, and let that cut heal. Like I said, no real harm done . . ." a perfect caesura . . . "except for the coat, that is."

In the bathroom of our small faculty apartment, the sadness comes. It hovers like a blue-tinged, woolly cloud. I stand before the mirror, staring at the blood-soaked collar and blood-spackled sleeves of my best winter coat, the only one I ever wear. "We'll get you another," Angie reassures me. "Right now, though, you need to get into bed."

"This is the coat *you* gave me," I say, "for our first Christmas together in Pittsburgh."

"I know, but—it's getting ragged anyway. You've already lost a button, and—"

"It's green. I just love that it's green. So all winter I go around thinking how the spring will come, how the green is only hidden underground."

"There are other green coats," she sighs, "and other times to mourn the loss of this one."

"You think you're making light, but you're not. It *is* a loss. This is my very first grown-up coat, the first substantial thing not purchased for me by my parents. I always think of it as my Can't-Go-Back coat, my This-Is-Who-I-Am-Now coat."

Her arm outstretched, quietly commanding my surrender. "Clothes wear out, you know. Everything does. I thought with all your flair for melodrama you might at least appreciate that this coat made such a grand finale."

Still clutching the worn green fabric around my shoulders, I walk to bed reciting, *"For the sword outwears its sheath, / And the soul wears out the breast, / And the heart must pause to breathe, / And love itself have rest."*

"Come on, Lord Byron," drawing back the quilt. "Put down thy head on yon pillow."

Autumn 1996.

Of all the holidays, I loved Halloween best: reveling in our finest disguises, slipping freely into any alternative self. But this particular Halloween represented for us a threshold we had long dreaded crossing over. The next year, at college, we couldn't be sure—self-conscious, sorority parties or passing out candy in the dorms? None of the old rituals then, our neighborhood pranks and shenanigans under the streetlights, our years of exceptional trespass through those countless, immaculate yards.

We only knew we would be leaving for a world half-imagined and mostly imagined wrong, its fodder and fluff poached from '90s sitcoms and *Lifetime* moment-of-truth movies.

But the part we got right—the part we intuitively understood even as we planned with fanfare all those future reunions that never took place—was the fact that we would be different when we returned. Some essential balance was destined to shift, was already shifting, and we were standing now on a fragile precipice, our last patch of common ground.

"Do you have the provisions?" I ask April, my best friend since fifth grade.

"Three cans of highly projectile spray cheese, check." She winks at me and tucks her bangs beneath the red satin headband with the glue-gunned devil horns.

"Ok then, here's the plan. As soon as Joy gets here, you'll ring the doorbell, and she and I will hide in the bushes. When Mr. Ronish comes out, your job is to lure him down the front walk; then Joy and I will jump him from behind."

"What am I supposed to tell him? You know he'll be suspicious."

"Tell him—tell him some kids graffitied his driveway, something scandalous and profane. You noticed it on your way to Joy's house and thought you should stop and let him know."

April nods. "By the way, I like your pirate costume."

"Thanks. I wish I had a parrot, though—and a peg leg."

"Did your parents act weird that we were getting dressed up, since we're far too old for trick-or-treat?"

"My parents always act weird. I'm not sure it was because of the costume."

From the curve of the cul-de-sac, swishing through the misty darkness, we see our friend Joy, my first friend from the neighborhood, maybe my first friend ever. "Who is she supposed to be? Little Red Riding Hood?" As Joy passes under the streetlights, her swing coat with the high felt collar appears first candy apple, then dusty rose, then blazes all at once superhero scarlet.

"By the way," April murmurs before taking off up the walk, "I changed my mind. I decided I'm *not* applying to college after all."

Joy and I huddle together behind the holly bushes, the ones with the sharp, star-shaped leaves and little red berries that poison the birds.

"What did I miss?" she asks.

I thrust a can of spray cheese into her hand. "April says she's not going to college."

Joy considers my words while swiftly braiding her hair, then tucks the thick rope of tightly wound curls inside the neck of her sweater. "That's silly. How does she think she's ever going to get laid?"

"Joy!" I don't know which friend has astonished me more. "I've never heard you talk that way before."

"Well, we don't spend as much time together as we used to," she sighs, "but don't worry. I'm not doing it—*yet*. I would tell you if I were."

"But I mean—going to college isn't about having sex. It's about choosing your career, building a good life for yourself."

"You must *really* trust your college counselor," Joy grins, half-serious, half-mocking. "C'mon, I think sex is part of a good life. I've been giving it a lot of thought lately, and I'm pretty sure my life would be better if I were having it."

"Who do you want to have it with?" My voice chafes with unbidden exasperation.

"I don't know. Lots of people, I guess." I raise my eyebrows. "Not all at once, but . . . *sequentially*."

"This is too much! April's not going to college, and you're planning orgies in your dorm room."

"Please! I said not all at once."

April and Mr. Ronish are still chatting on the porch. She is trying to sound casual, like she's not in a hurry, but I can see her finger pulsing on the can of spray cheese she clasps behind her back.

"So, are you Little Red Riding Hood?" I ask Joy, my voice softened by sudden melancholy.

"No. I'm Parisian. I'm a gay Parisian lady—not *gay*, but gay, like light, merry. A high-society, art-collector type. Probably the mistress of the head curator at the Louvre." I roll my eyes at this second suggestion of Joy's burgeoning nymphomania.

"You don't need to be somebody's *mistress*. Why don't *you* be the head curator at the Louvre?"

"Listen!" She holds a finger over my lips. "This costume is completely authentic. My mother's mother bought her this coat on a trip to Paris thirty years ago. And now she's given it to me."

"For Halloween?"

"For anytime. For . . . *dressing up*."

"Then it's not really much of a costume, is it? Not if you're only playing yourself."

Joy is about to retort, but then we see Mr. Ronish in his faded jeans and fur-trimmed house shoes sauntering down the drive. April has ducked behind the garbage cans and is motioning for us to *go now! this is your big chance!* But before we can leap out from our hiding place, we're sabotaged. Mr. Ronish steps back, wrests the spray can from April's unguarded hand, and lunges full-force toward us, shooting long strands of liquefied cheese into our faces and hair, the full length of our squirming, shuddering bodies.

April is laughing in spite of herself, and I am fighting back the best I am able, but Joy has stopped struggling and lays flat on the ground, her eyes closed, quietly sobbing. "Are you hurt? Did I hurt you?" Mr. Ronish calls out with concern.

Joy shakes her head, eyes still closed, chest heaving.

He looks at me and wiggles his mustache. "I've been

watching you girls out here for the last twenty minutes. I let April string me along a little, but I couldn't just roll over and play dead." Then, slugging my shoulder in a good-natured way: "I figured *you* were the mastermind behind this operation, so I hope I cheesed you up the most."

"Yeah, looks like you got me pretty good," I concede.

"Well, if you get things sorted out and yourselves cleaned up, you can come back later for dessert. I don't know what Patty's baking, but it sure as hell smells good."

April and I sit down on the pavement, one of us on either side of Joy. "Do you want to sit up?" I nudge. She shakes her head. "C'mon, you're just adding damp and grime to cheese."

What happened? April mouths the words to me, but before I can answer, Joy opens her eyes and snaps, "No! I've heard about enough out of you."

"This isn't *my* fault," I reply, incredulous.

"Oh, no? Whose juvenile idea was it to spray cheese on our neighbor?"

"Well, who thinks the point of college is illicit sex?"

"I never said *illicit*. I don't even know what that means."

April raises a tenuous hand. "Can one of you *please* tell me what's going on?"

"This is my mother's coat from Paris, and now it's ruined." Joy tugs the braid free from her sweater and slowly begins to unravel her curls.

"Maybe, with a good dry-cleaning—"

"Yeah, maybe." But it's clear to us that Joy has given up already.

"It's still a really nice coat," April offers, petting the hemline as if it were a dog.

"And you're not going to college," I say. "So you've got something ruined, too."

"What?"

"Your life, that's what."

"Oh, please!" Joy exclaims. "There's more than one way to

get out of the house. And there's certainly more than one way to be happy."

"*Exactly.* I'll get a job and an apartment, and then, maybe in a few years when I have a better idea about what I want to do, I'll look into college."

Now I find that I'm the one who's sulking, scraping cheese off my tight, striped pants and biting my lip to hold back tears.

"The key is to make connections with people," Joy instructs in her worst, know-it-all voice. "Join a social group or a community center. The last thing you want is to end up a recluse."

"I thought the worst thing according to you was to end up a virgin," I grouse.

"That too," Joy says, suddenly rising and unbuttoning her coat despite the chill.

"Where is all this sex talk coming from?" April looks at me like it must be my doing. I tear the bandana off my head and spring to my feet in protest.

"Joy's the one—she's the one who started all of it. Or you are—with your great big college cop-out."

"I'm *not* copping out—I'm just not ready. And I know I'm not, and I *won't* let you make me feel bad about it." April turns around twice, to look at both of us, then starts off down the street.

"But we're friends!" I call after her.

"That's what *I* thought!" Her voice floats back to me on the breeze.

"So, what? I'm a bad friend now—just because I want people to do their best, not sell themselves short?" I shake the bangles one by one from my wrists and shove them deep in my cheese-covered bag.

"No," Joy sighs. "You're just a really hard person to let down easy."

"What does that mean?"

"It means nobody likes to disappoint you, but most of us feel like we're bound to."

"Even you?"

Joy wraps a generous arm around my shoulder, stands up on her tip-toes, and kisses my cheek. "Do me a favor, every once in a while." We are walking toward her house, which glows like a luminaria in the dark—the kind we used to make in grade school: *take a paper bag, cut out some stars, fill the bottom with sand, light a candle.*

"Sure. What?" I am trying to look straight ahead and not let my bottom lip quiver.

"Don't just do it for me either—do it for you. Every once in a while, let yourself be absolutely devastated."

"What?"

She is wearing the coat like a cape now, with only the collar secured and her hands free and gesturing like shadow puppets above the gleaming puddles. "So you'll know the difference between being let down and being destroyed."

Then, she is off, a red-orange arabesque streaking the solemn dark. "That's some real hippie bullshit!" I holler after her. But I stand a long time, one foot on the sidewalk, one foot in the road, before I bend my body westward and head home.

Winter 1988.

When I was a child growing up in the Pacific Northwest, winters were exceedingly mild. If you wanted snow, you drove up into the mountains—Snoqualmie Summit or Stevens Pass or Alpental—some place you could ski and sled, then sit back and watch your breath rise: thick, ghostly smokestacks to the stars.

There we are—the little blue car pulled over on the shoulder. That's my father, squatting on the ice in his snow boots, binding chains to our fat, black tires. And there, on the passenger side, scripting the grocery list in her perfect penmanship—lots of curls and cues and many coupons—that's my mother. I'm in the back seat: tall for my age, bookish but talkative. The condensation kisses on the windows are my doing.

"It used to be when I was a child," my father says, opening the door and blowing hard on his hands—"

"Bill, you're letting the heat out!"

"Oh, sorry." He climbs inside and revs the engine, winking at me in the rearview mirror.

"Bill, stop it. You're just showing off, and it's not good for the car."

"It used to be, Julie, when I was a child, growing up in the great state of Montana—"

"Are we going or what? You pay the same price for a day or an hour."

"Do you mind if I finish a thought here?"

"Do you think you could think and drive?"

I lean my head forward and make a bridge with my hands, elbows spread between the bucket seats. "What were you saying, Dad?"

"When I was about your age, we lived in Billings, Montana, and the winters there were unbelievably rough. Imagine waking up every morning to this stuff, right in your own backyard!"

"I'd love it!" I beam. "And every year we'd have a white Christmas, guaranteed."

"You'd get sick of it soon enough," my mother insists. "Now, speaking of Christmas, shall we do a run-through of your recitation?"

"Ok," I agree, clearing my throat. "*'Twas the night before Christmas—*"

"Title and author first, please."

"Oh right—'The Night Before Christmas' by Clement Moore. *'Twas the night before Christmas—*"

"Look at those icicles!" my father exclaims, gesturing to a row of crystalline swords dangling from a deer crossing sign.

"Bill, we're practicing here, if you don't mind."

"Can we have some Christmas carols?" I request, jutting my head between them once again.

"Sure. Do you want Roger Whittaker or Bette Midler?"

"Hands on the wheel, Bill," my mother commands. "Julie, you should have picked your cassette tapes before we left home. This isn't a good time for your father to be searching through that overhead compartment of his."

"Well, we don't have to play music; we could sing our own songs."

"Why don't we review some of your spelling words? It'll be bee season before you know it, and I just happen to have the *Seattle Times* official word list with me," she says, laying the newspaper like a napkin across her lap.

"Ok. Don't go in alphabetical order. Surprise me." I lick my lips for a good luck taste of cherry gloss.

"*Deciduous.*"

"Deciduous," I repeat with trepidation. "D-e-c. . . . Could you use it in a sentence please?"

"You're stalling."

"But you're allowed to!"

"Unlike coniferous trees, *deciduous* trees lose their leaves every autumn, and they don't grow back until the following spring."

"What's an example of a deciduous tree?"

"Stalling."

"No, really, I want to know."

"Montana was full of deciduous trees," my father interjects proudly. "We had oaks and maples and birches, and there were these cottonwood trees—"

"Nobody is interested in a botany lesson, Bill."

"*I* am," plaintively rocking.

"You've never even been there, Linda. How long have we been talking about taking the train—"

"Are you kicking the seat?" my mother demands, her eyes brimming bright with blue fire.

"Sorry. It's just—are we almost there?"

"What did we say about that question?"

"That it's annoying and impertinent and we'll get there when we get there."

"Correct. And when we get there, what are you *not* going to do?"

"Jump out of the car and go running all around without my coat on."

"Good. *Deciduous.*"

"So it means dying, but with the potential for reincarnation?"

"*Spell it.*"

"D-e-c . . ." gazing out the window again, leaning over to smooch the glass, then meeting my mother's disapproving eyes in the mirror, and sitting up straight again "i-d-u . . ." choking in a quick breath — "o-u-s."

"Correct!" She sounds pleased, and I feel my toes uncoil in the snug fleece of my boots.

"Hey Mom, why are these called *moon boots?*"

"I haven't the faintest idea."

"Well, why do we have to wear the hard boots to ski? I like the soft ones so much better."

"We're here!" my father proclaims. "Set your dials for excitement, women of the family Wade!"

"Park over there. I don't want a bunch of college kids flinging open their doors and dinging us." My mother checks her makeup in a hand-held mirror, then rummages through her pocket for a candy.

"Can I have one?"

"I don't know — *can* you?"

"If you give me one, I can!" My mother flashes me a tight-lipped frown, but on the driver's side, I hear my father chuckle.

What we discover when we climb out of the car is that my father has brought me last year's parka. "She's outgrown it, Bill. Didn't I clearly explain? *This* bag" — holding it up like a fish about to be tossed — "is going to Goodwill. What happened to the new coat and gloves that I set at the top of the stairs?"

He shakes his head, the color of salt with a dash of pepper. My mother says he is prematurely gray. "I don't know, Linda. I'm sorry. I thought I brought everything you asked."

"Does this mean I can ski without a coat?" I plead, dropping to my knees and folding my prayer-hands dramatically.

"Get up!" my mother snaps. "Why must you always make a scene? Now here's what we're going to do. I'll wear your father's coat, and you'll wear my coat. You'll be fine, won't you, Bill?"

"Oh, sure. I've got my long underwear and a couple of sweaters here."

"Don't be modest," she says, with a sharp jab to his gut. "There's an extra thirty pounds there that are bound to keep you warm. Keep eating the way you do, and you'll have enough blubber to insulate a whale."

My father has a kind face and creased cheeks from where he holds his smile as hard as he can for as long as he can. Now I watch him wince and turn away.

"Your coat is too big on me," I tell my mother, as she zips me up brusquely and steps back to admire.

"You'll grow into it. That's what people do."

"I look like I'm wearing a garbage bag," I grumble. "Or like a prune that's still wearing its skin from before it was shrunk."

"That doesn't even make sense. Now come on!" she chides, fastening my ticket to my new pruny uniform. "I think we're ready for an intermediate run. Bill, what are you doing? Feeding your face? Well, I'm taking Julie up to Dodge Ridge."

"I don't know, Linda. She's only ever done the rope tow. If you want to ski Dodge, I can take her for a run on the bunny slopes."

"No, I think she's ready," my mother says. "What do you think?"

I nod, knowing what is expected of me. "Daddy, I want to sit next to you on the chair lift."

"Oh, I see. So *I'm* supposed to ride with a stranger?"

He winces again; his eyes dart away, then return. "Tell you what, Julie. You ride up with your mom this time. She'll help you get the hang of it. And then, maybe later, we'll take a ride. . . ." He has his hard boots on now; so do I.

The coat is too big for me, but I find that if I hunker down deep enough, so the collar comes over my nose, it screens out the wind and drowns out the sound of my mother's voice reciting my father's wrongs. "When I married him, he weighed a hundred sixty-five pounds—can you imagine?" She has her goggles propped on her head, but I keep mine down so she can't watch the way my eyes wander, roaming the landscape, traversing the trails lined with evergreens, which from this vantage look hardly larger than the little green sprigs we wrap in gauze and call our Christmas village. "What if I had gained that much weight? How would *he* like it? What if I had packed that many pounds onto *my* frame?"

I am trying not to wonder. I am clinging to the pole that separates my mother's chair from my chair on this tram without windows or walls, and I am trying not to wonder about the number of people every year who fall . . . some by accident, some by prank or malice, and some who surely don't fall at all—who see something they want, some little sprig of green popping up from that barren, icy topography—but go after it, drop into it, *look before they leap* and keep looking all the way down.

"Now when we get up there, I want you to scoot to the edge of the seat and push off from it. Wait till I tell you. You can hold your poles in one hand if you need to, but we're just going to glide right down that little hill over there, and then we'll stop and collect ourselves."

She has her goggles on her forehead like a second set of eyes, which makes me think of Riding Hood and the Wolf— *the better to see you with, my dear.* Her cheeks are red and wind-burned, and I can tell the dismount makes her nervous.

"All right now, on three. *One . . . two . . . three.*" She pushes off from her chair, and she glides down the hill, but I am not beside her or behind. In the distance, my mother is screaming my name, but I sink low in the coat and pretend not to hear.

On the way down the mountain in my single chair, skis gently swinging below, I see my father. He too is alone, watching the trees pass under his feet, these evergreens smocked in white like chefs or surgeons. The white seems to give them a sense of purpose.

At first, he doesn't recognize me, a shriveled-up plum in a pruny disguise, too many layers of poly-blend and nylon. Then, he does, and his mouth gapes—my father inching his way up the mountain and I inching my way back down—but, though our eyes meet and our lips part with some kind of special intention, neither of us utters a sound.

What was the right word then—what do you think—for two deciduous points on that line?

Traveling

Summer 2002. Butte, Montana. Harrison Avenue Plaza.

The last time I called my father was from a sticky pay phone outside a LensCrafters store in the midst of a heavily air-conditioned Montana mall. Now only a time zone apart, I had stopped there—in the valley of the Richest Hill on Earth—to try to reach him. Through the bright transparent doors gleaming with fingerprints, I watched Angie pace. She had quit smoking a few days before, and as she moved back and forth across the smoldering pavement, her fingers flicked a nonexistent cigarette.

"Dad?"

Though he had but one child, he hesitated, unsure of the name and the woman who pronounced it. Then, anxious: "Is everything all right?"

No, it's fucking hot here, and I hate Montana already. What I said, what I had been trained to say: "Of course. Everything's fine. You'll never guess where I'm calling you from."

Angie peered in through the smudged glass, smiled.

"Somewhere unlikely, I guess. Have you checked in with your mother, by the way?"

"I'm in *Butte*, Dad. I didn't want to tell you, in case my course changed, but I've been planning to stop here since I set out on this trip, and later today I'm headed on to Billings."

All my life my father had talked about taking the train to Montana, back to the city of his birth and that other city, Billings, where he was raised until the age of eleven. Butte he couldn't quite remember, but Billings he wore like a comfortable coat, slipping into its soft roomy fabric with each autumn's shift toward winter. *It was a different life there, winters like you wouldn't believe. We were kids. We loved the snow, frolicked in it till we were numb, and come summer. . . .* Here he'd trail off in a faint ellipsis of image: *cottonwood trees, "King of the Mountain," that endless sky.*

In 1953, my grandfather took a job with Goodyear, moving his young family farther west—to the misty chill and mild manners of Washington State. They made their home in Seattle, a new development overlooking Puget Sound, where short rows of tidy matchbox houses ornamented the otherwise deserted hills. *Your Aunt Linda cried and cried. She said she could never love a place the way she loved Montana. Me—I was ready to move on. Another big adventure. I was my father's son.*

"Butte. Really? How 'bout that? Do you have a camera with you?"

"Yes. I promise I'll take pictures."

"And you say you're going to stop in Billings? Are you sure it's not out of your way?"

It was, but— "No, no, not at all. Where should we go while we're there?"

He stuttered, stopped. My pronouns were showing again. I had not been traveling alone, or lightly. This he knew. I had not called my mother since Sheridan, Wyoming, where I was terse and noncompliant, hanging up on her mid-question before she dissolved into tears. This he knew also.

"Bruce Street, where we lived," he recovered slowly. "The

house number was 4602. And, if you think of it—if there's time—the Garfield School."

Angie motioned to the soda machine, and I nodded my head. Following with my eyes, I felt the slow burn, the palm-wet longing of a love still new: her zippered pockets, her dusty blue shoes.

"And Julie," he pleaded—"one more thing."

Angie unraveled a one-dollar bill and stretched it taut against the wall to smooth the wrinkles. My eyes mesmerized: long line of her back, stacked vertebrae my fingers ascended and descended with purposeless pleasure.

"Sure, Dad. What?"

"Have a heart. Call your mother."

August 5, 2002. Seaside, Oregon. The Tides Motel. Recycled Paper. (Unsent)

Dear Dad, I'm up late, listening to the ocean, trying to memorize the precise intonations of the waves. But I'll forget them, of course. I always do. That's part of the allure of this place, wouldn't you say?

It's your anniversary today, and you've spent it as you always do: arguing with Mom over clam linguine and trying to impress the wide-eyed waitress at the Old Spaghetti Factory. What's the new plan? Have you decided yet? Faith-based intervention or at-home exorcism? Don't think I don't know what you're fighting about most these days.

You burn me up, you know that? You really do. I remember when I was a kid, and Mom used to say that to me. I just "burned her up," made her so angry she had no choice but to slap me or scream. She called it "swatting"—one hard slap, hard as she could, with no immediate repetition, because that would be "spanking," and only "low-class people" spanked their kids. But you don't know about the swats, do you? You don't know about the screaming either. (Don't know, or don't want to?) You were on the road all week, and I don't blame you for that, Dad. You didn't have to quit for me. What you could have done was just the opposite: you could have taken me with you.

Yes, Dad, I'm angry. I'm burning up. I'm here at the end of the Lewis and Clark Trail, and I'd just as soon turn around and follow it all the way back to St. Louis than drive the last five hours up the Coast to where you are. I have your pictures, and half of me wants to go down to the shore right now and shuck them all in the outgoing tide. We were supposed to go there together—to Montana. You always said we would, and she vetoed. Why did Mom call all the shots? Why does she still? But you raised me too well, Dad. I'll put on a happy face and a pretty dress, and I'll be home in time for my birthday. I'm not coming alone, though. Remember that. Why did it have to turn out this way? What happened to the two of us in our cowboy hats and all your pioneer promises?

1953–1971. Seattle, Washington. Fauntlee Hills. (Home Base)

I come from a long line of traveling salesmen. They are trustworthy, approachable men who love a Protestant God cut from their own moderate, clean-shaven cloth. Their vices include Jimmy Stewart westerns, penny ante poker, and thick slices of banana cream pie topped off with a tall cup of coffee, no matter what the time of day. They wear nondescript suits and carry thin briefcases and beige trench coats draped loosely over their arms. They are tall, dark, and handsome. They always hold doors and walk on the curbside. They speak remarkably well about the weather.

Grandpa John, my father's father, sold tires, belts, hoses, and air springs for Goodyear for eighteen years. Before that, other products for other companies. It wasn't the product his clients sought to purchase after all; rather, his *confidence* in the product, his persuasive faith. Imagine that firm handshake, that sincere smile, the competent and detailed explanations he provided each listening ear. Good-looking, but not slick. Attentive, but not fawning. They were paying to be *like* him, to espouse their own unshakeable conviction in something as simple as rubber—perhaps a primer for something abstract as love, authoritative as religion. "Johnny genuinely liked people," my grandmother reminisced. "And people genuinely liked Johnny. It was a useful—and profitable—exchange."

Or: "He could sell an icebox to an Eskimo," as my father was fond of saying.

They were long days though, hours cresting the windshield in shadowed increments. The sturdy dashboard of this Ford or that Oldsmobile, littered with hand-scrawled notes and battered Interstate maps. How did he pass that time? In an era before tape decks, let alone mobile phones, the poor radio reception across the Great Plains and later, down the Coastal Highway. . . . Was he telling stories to himself, dreaming sensational plots of murder, mayhem, or something softer—a sentimental romance with too many possible endings to ever keep count? (Some of them happy, some of them not. . . .) He ate alone at greasy spoons and truck stops, tipped generously, scoured the paper for memorable comics, and never left an empty square on a single crossword page. But I'm greedy. I want more. If you had seen this man through a rain-streaked diner window some sultry Wichita twilight, or come upon him unloading his suitcase from a blue Pontiac with out-of-state plates, red tail of a motel key peeking from his back trouser pocket, what would you have surmised? A *good* man? *Kind? Simple? Dull?* What drumbeat of adjectives might have thumped through your skull as he slipped past you—touching his hat, nodding his greeting, perhaps humming a tune from the Big Band era—into that infinite dark?

Summer 2002. Billings, Montana. Cracker Barrel Restaurant. South Frontage Road and Interstate 90.

We arrived in Billings at dusk, wily child of sun peering out from behind the crooked rocks. I turned the wheel softly under my hand, as if I knew where I was going and needn't rush.

"So, here we are"—to christen the moment we had backtracked 200 miles to claim. Sprawling around us like a ransacked room: this largest city in Montana, this Magic City, land my father first called home.

"I'm hungry. Wonder what's good." Angie's long fingers strumming the dash.

"Well, I did see a sign about a mile back for—"

"Oh, God. Aren't you sick of that place yet?"

"It's *comfort* food. How can you turn down comfort food at the end of a long day on the road?" We eyed each other in the grainy dark. "And don't forget about their homemade tortilla soup and lemon icebox pie. . . ."

Her face: sweat-streaked, sepia-shadowed. Under her breath, consenting.

"What was that?"

"You heard me."

"I'm not sure—"

"Take the exit!"

My face: sweat-streaked, smiling.

Cracker Barrel restaurants weren't in business back when my grandfather roved the country in his company car, singing church hymns a cappella and practicing his punch lines. By the time my father took to the highways in the 1970s, this home-style cooking chain had begun to flourish, though mostly in the Southern states: Tennessee, the Carolinas, Georgia. To this day, there are no Cracker Barrels in Washington, Oregon, or California, so I never chanced upon their fresh-baked biscuits with warm apple butter, or their hash brown casserole thickened with cheese, or their fried okra and white bean vegetable sampler during my childhood travels. It took this trip, with

Angie, just weeks before my twenty-third birthday, for the restaurant first opened in her native Tennessee to cross my path and become my hands-down favorite.

"They're not fond of our kind here, you know," she reminded as we passed the row of Hinkle rocking chairs—adult-sized and child-sized, each one handmade—toward the double wooden doors.

Angie had grown up with Cracker Barrel as an old standard, the "local flavor" she had had just about enough of. It was one thing, being a tourist, a sightseer—whatever we were—but quite another when Cracker Barrel sat (*loomed*) in your own backyard. Breakfast, lunch, *and* dinner. Before *and* after church. In Tennessee, Cracker Barrel was as sacred and familiar as whiskey or religion, and while the restaurants weren't licensed to serve the former, the taste of God and good country values permeated every tabletop and over-portioned entree right up to the elk heads on the dark cedar walls.

"I don't see how it's possible for a lesbian to like this place."

A young waitress named Jonelle with four gold stars adorning her apron guided us toward a corner table. "Did you see that? She's got four. That must mean she's very good."

"Or very *trapped*. I think you earn a star for every year you work here."

"Who says I'm a lesbian, by the way? I rather resent that," flashing a coy smile and unrolling the shiny fork, knife, and spoon from their paper cocoon.

"Can I get you girls something to drink while you look over the menus?"

"Coffee, please," Angie replied. "Two." Then, reaching for the famous peg game, Cracker Barrel equivalent of a Rubik's Cube: "What? At least their coffee's good."

So we sat in the ginger-soft light, each table equipped with a lantern. We ate hearty made-from-scratch foods—perhaps flapjacks this time with "tree-tapped" syrup, or country ham and biscuits soaked in gravy. And we talked as if the loud crow of the rooster wall clock meant nothing. Around us: young men withdrew wallets from overall pockets while the girls they were with gazed back at them gratefully. Ash trays overflowed with fine-ground Winstons, Salems, the occasional Virginia Slim. Babies burped and wailed at high volume.

As Angie was quick to point out, there always *were* a lot of babies at the Cracker Barrel, causing a ruckus in their old-fashioned high chairs and booster seats brightly red-vinyled. "Babies and queer-hating Republicans—just some of your typical clientele."

I watched her fingers fondle the ashtray longingly, return to the peg game in progress. "Don't forget about the squirrel hunters," I teased.

Her eyes bright as flame: "Them too."

Outside the night waited: remote city without reservations, cell phone reception shoddy at best. I sat back, heart swooning, smile wide.

"What are you grinning about?"

"Nothing."

"You have a plan for tomorrow—where to start at least?"

"Not really."

"Well, you think you might need one?" Nimbly picking off peg after peg: pattern identified, turning to rote.

"Probably will."

Our eyes met then, above the flux and din of strangers, the scrape of silverware. And all at once, we burst into laughter.

1974–1986. Seattle, Washington. Fauntlee Hills. (Home Base)

In the old days, when my father sold paper and packaging products, first for Crown Zellerbach and later for the Bemis Company, I waited all week for our Friday night trips to the airport. My mother and I sat at the dinner table, my chair tipped back just far enough to read the blue digits on the microwave clock. They never changed fast enough. Around seven, she would call the airport to confirm my father's estimated arrival time while I hurriedly scuttled the last of the peas across my plate.

"Where is he flying from today?" I'd ask.

Terra Haute, Indiana, if this had been a big sales trip, or *Boise, Idaho,* if only for marketing meetings, or any of a dozen other cities where he consulted with old clients, recruited new, and collected my requested hand lotions and hotel stationery from one or several Holiday Inns. Twist-top pens imprinted with hotel name, city, and logo were an intermittent luxury, as were prepackaged shower caps and mini-shampoos smelling like strawberry Quik or violets.

Then, pushing away my empty plate, I'd contemplate the map of the United States (with Alaska and Hawaii set off to the side and emphatically *NOT DRAWN TO SCALE*). This was my placemat, denoting capital cities and state lines, each nameable region shaded with one of six vibrant colors. I had cars also, for vicarious travel, borrowed from a racetrack my father had set up in the basement—the same racetrack my mother protested for putting "boyish ideas" into my head. But I wasn't interested in racing per se. That was my father's idea. What interested me was driving: what might be glimpsed from the ground up in this massive sprawl called America, this place I claimed as "my favorite country" and my "country of origin."

It was the waiting I loathed, standing outside in a reversible raincoat while my mother backed her Pinto station wagon down the drive. "Bet I could do that for you," I'd murmur, thinking she couldn't hear.

"You're six years old! Do you want me to get arrested?"

Next, she cautiously withdrew my father's fine, shiny company car—one of many over the years—from where we kept it (covered, protected) between the teetering carport walls. This Buick or Crown Victoria she inched forward and emergency-braked in front of our neighbor's yard. Jumping out again, her impractical shoes sloshing in the downpour, umbrella inconsistent over her head, she'd pull her own car into the carport and motion for me to climb into the back seat of my father's.

No sitting up front. Not until I was older. Fourteen at least. *No exceptions*. Except she didn't know on Saturday afternoons, my father ferried me about town as his copilot, turning the dials haphazardly, blasting us cool and then warm.

"Do you love your father more than me?" Her steely eyes fixed to the road but glanced back at regular intervals to study my face in the rearview mirror.

"What do you mean?" I'd stumble.

"Don't play dumb, Rainbow Brite. You know *exactly* what I mean."

"Of course not. You're my parents," pattern identified, turning to rote: "I love you both the same."

"If we got divorced—your father and I—which of us would you rather live with?"

And the answer was easy, of course, because I *did* love my father more (even then) and felt ashamed of myself for it.

"You know, when I was a child, my mother loved me the least of her three children. She seemed to wish she had never had me at all."

"I'm sorry," I'd whisper.

"Are you, Julie? Because you sure don't act like it. How do you think it makes me feel to see you barely able to contain your delight at a phone call from your father, putting on your coat and shoes two or three hours before his plane even departs—as if you could will him here faster."

Helplessly: "I just miss him, that's all."

"Would you miss me if *I* were gone?" Her lips pursed, her knuckles straining white against the wheel.

"You mean, if *you* were a traveling salesman?"

I let the possibility sweep through me: weeknights boiling hot dogs on the stove, Mariners baseball on television, ironing my father's shirts and spraying them with starch until they crisped up to their bright-white collars. The long drives we would take along the water, down to the lighthouse at Alki Point and over the bridge into the city. More practice with my tennis serve, my catcher's mitt, and best of all, driving his company car through the car wash—the Pink Elephant car wash downtown—where sometimes my father lifted me into the driver's seat as the windshield vanished under seven layers of soap and the rough scrub of two enormous sponges rocked us like an amusement park ride.

For that moment, I indulged the fantasy of a world where my mother was expendable, replaceable; a world where I could fill her tall, implacable shoes so efficiently my father wouldn't even notice she had disappeared.

"I mean, if I were gone *permanently*. If I *died*."

I leaned against the cold upholstery, green or gray in the dim light. Swish of the windshield wipers and my mother's eyes trained on mine. *How long till I saw my father again? Were there hours left, or merely minutes?*

"Of course I'd miss you, Mom."

"More than you'd miss your father?"

The tall, slender man in the trench coat, standing curbside, rolling luggage and garment bag, waving his one free hand. *Was it possible I could love anyone more?*

Silent, I slumped down in my seat. Guilty, I gazed out the window.

June 28, 2003. Albuquerque, New Mexico. Intown-Suites. Hotel Stationery. (unsent)

> *Dear Dad, I've had a nightmare, the kind you can't get back to sleep from, no matter how hard you try. It was about you. I dreamed you had a heart attack, and Mom wasn't home. I was the only person who could have saved you, but I failed. When the paramedics came, they asked why I hadn't tried CPR, and I told them I had, but they didn't believe me. They called me "careless." They asked me if I even had a heart at all. "If he dies," they said, "it'll be on your conscience forever."*
>
> *I don't know if you died in the dream or not, but I woke up paralyzed with fear. Angie said I was shaking but wouldn't*

open my eyes. I wanted to stay there, in that hospital room, holding your hand until someone in a white coat pronounced you safely "out of the woods." But when the dream's closing credits began to roll, I felt myself snatched out of your life, the white light pulling me instead toward my future. And by the time you get this letter, you'll know the truth. You'll know that I'm gone for good.

We've been on the road almost a week now. The little apartment in Bellingham — rented out to someone else who smokes weed and feeds the seagulls from her kitchen window. We packed up everything we owned (and a few things we're still paying for) in our old Ford wagon that week. I told you we'd gone kayaking in the San Juans. Time for a clean break. I couldn't risk Mom's hysterics, and I wasn't sure I was strong enough to make any face-to-face good-byes. Angie's looking for work, and I have a lead on a writing program in Pittsburgh. Plus, come summer — I don't know what it is — I get this hankering. I want to be out on the road again, seeing all there is to see.

Does this make me a runaway, you think? Does this make me a coward? I can't help feeling — forgive the pun — "driven to it," like if I didn't exile myself, someone else was going to do it for me. I had surgery a few weeks back. Doctors slit open my throat, removed my thyroid. Lots of little tumors: not malignant yet, but trying. I thought about you before they put me under. I thought how I used to be afraid to put my head beneath the water, how I cried at your insistence that I jump into the deep end. "Be brave!" you'd shout, and I was — not because of some surplus courage, but because I couldn't bear to disappoint you. That's how it was in the operating room. I feared the anesthesia; I feared the lost time, the absent memory. I feared sinking too deep, drowning. What I dreamed: that I was Sleeping Beauty, and Angie came to kiss me, and when I opened my eyes, I knew at once I didn't have to choose between you. She wasn't a prince, but she could still be my lover; you were still my father, but you had learned it was possible to also be my friend.

We're leaving New Mexico this morning, heading on through Texas, Oklahoma, and into Arkansas. I'm excited to see these new places that were once only squares on a placemat to me. Ask me any capital. I know them all, sure as the back of my hand. Wish I knew you that way, Dad. Wish you knew me.

Summer 2002. Billings, Montana. Picture Court Motel. Gulf Station.

Angie was up first, swathing her tattoo with sunscreen. A Celtic creature from the Lindisfarne Gospels, the artwork encircled a portion of upper arm, trapping—as legend told it—her eternal soul inside her mortal body.

"Looks good," I smiled, kissing her shoulder in passing.

"You don't think it's faded at all? I haven't been as careful as I should be."

"It looks"—peeking back around the corner, tongue resolutely in cheek—"as if your place in the afterlife might be unsecured."

"Ha, ha. They can have it. Hey—did you hear those motorcycles this morning?"

"Nope."

"Well, the Sturgis-bound crowd is in town, and chances are, they've cleared out most of the continental breakfasts."

"We'll get some coffee, tide us over till we can stop for brunch."

"In Montana?"

"*Yes*, in Montana."

"No buffets, ok?"

"Ok."

"And no Cracker Barrel."

Reluctantly: "I promise."

I'm superstitious about stopping at Gulf Stations since all the trouble started at one such fill-and-go establishment in *The Texas Chainsaw Massacre*. Nonetheless, when I saw the ancient Superman-style phone booth—size of a comfortable fitting room—in a Gulf parking lot on the outskirts of Billings, I took a chance and pulled over under the ominous orange sign.

"What are you doing?"

"I'm going to look through the phone book, see if there's a street directory."

"That's one option," Angie remarked, returned to reading her book.

"Can you think of anything better?"

"Well, even if you find the street, you're going to have to ask for directions. Why not ask the cashier if he knows where Bruce Street is and get directions at the same time?"

She was right, of course, though how I had relished the thought of standing inside that phone booth, preparing my symbolic transformation.

As I reached for my wallet and a Best Western pen, absconded with a couple states back, Angie intercepted my hand. "You don't have to do this, you know. You don't owe anybody anything, not even an explanation."

Metronome of my pulse holding me steady: "I just miss him, that's all."

"I know you do"—folding my fingers one by one—"but none of this brings him back."

Picture me stepping into the Gulf Station: ordinary girl— green t-shirt, light khakis, sandals. Apprehensive at first, glancing around for Leatherface, wary of the chainsaw's rev and buzz. Picture the man behind the counter: ordinary man, about my father's age—trim beard, graying hair, working the crossword page.

"Can I help you with anything, Miss?"

Scanning the shelves, I reach for a magazine (*Us Weekly*,

People, something like that), place it conciliatorily on the counter. "Yes, thank you."

"Anything else?"

"Some gum," I say, adding a pack of Doublemint.

"Anything else?"

Deep breath. "Just a question actually—about directions."

Picture the man removing his glasses, laying his mechanical pencil down. Do I seem nervous to him? Am I fidgeting the way a shady character would? Does he expect the worst of me?

"Well, where do you need to go?"

"I need to find Bruce Street," I say.

"Ain't no Bruce Street in Billings," he says, regarding me in a reserved but curious way.

"Are you sure?"

"I've lived here all my life, know this city like the back of my hand." We both consider it a moment: his pale knuckles, knobby and flecked with hairs; his dotted landscape of moles remote as country houses.

"Oh," I sigh, handing him money from my pocket. "Well, then."

"There is a Bruce *Avenue*, though. Residential street. Not more than five minutes from here heading north across the railroad tracks."

Picture my crestfallen face rising at the prospect. "That must be it."

"I can write down the roads you take to get there if you like," and I nodded. As he wrote, I felt my body unhinge beneath me, giddy and light. "Do you mind my asking what's so special about Bruce Avenue?"

Picture me looking up, beaming. This is my moment of glory, my chance to play the role I have always wanted to play: not a prodigal any longer, but a good and loving daughter—not the woman I am, treading this long, brambled path toward estrangement.

"My father was born here—well, in the state of Montana— and he was raised in Billings most of his childhood."

"Is that a fact?"

"He and my aunt and my grandparents—they lived on Bruce Street, or that's what they called it, so I'm headed there to see the house for myself. I hope it's still standing."

"Well, that's a mighty fine idea. I hope you and your sister brought a camera with you—take some pictures, for posterity's sake."

"My sister?"

"Young lady out there in the car," gesturing to Angie. "It's hard to miss a family resemblance like that."

"Oh, she's not—" But I stopped there. It was a moment that would return like instant replay for the rest of my life: all those false assumptions, those sisterly presumptions. Though we looked nothing alike, strangers sensed a familiarity between us, a peaceable comfort only manifest in those who loved each other deeply, who shared an intimate bond.

"Yes," I smiled, backing away slowly, sensing again my foreignness, even here on my father's terrain. "We have a camera."

"Your daddy's a lucky man, his girls driving clear across— where are those plates from now?" as he craned his neck toward the window.

Me, meekly: "Washington."

"All the way from Washington to visit his origins. I tell you what; that's devotion."

I would learn this reaction, come to dread it despite the lure of easy affirmation. The man behind the counter had warmed to me. I had kindled him with my lies—or rather, with my complicity in his storytelling. I had given him permission to make me whoever he wanted me to be.

Thanksgiving, 1997. Seattle, Washington. Park-n-Ride Parking Lot. West Marginal Way.

"Now don't repeat this, but your mother was never much of a driver. For one thing, she uses her right foot for the gas and her left foot for the brake, and she's trapped by that. She can forget about ever learning to drive stick."

My father had taken me out on a deserted holiday morning steeped in fog to begin (two years late) my automotive education. He had been waiting, he said, until the time was right, and now—a freshman in college, living away—my time had become less his own to claim.

"You're book-smart, and that's fine, but it has nothing to do with the road. In fact, it could hurt you in the long run if you don't develop some intuitive skills. Because that's the thing with driving, Julie: I can teach you all the rules, but it won't be enough. There's so much you'll have to learn on your own."

Conversations with my father tended to proceed this way, aphorisms accumulating like pebbles in his hand. We stood together, always on the shore of something greater, toeing the water with our words. As he once taught me to skip stones across the light skin of Puget Sound, hardly making an indentation, I learned from him also the best way to resolve a conflict was never to acknowledge it had existed at all. *Don't break the surface.*

"Remember when I was a kid, and you made me practice jumping in the deep end at Colman Pool, and that was preparation for diving—head-first—and the diving was preparation for swimming all the way to the bottom and touching it, just to prove I could?"

My father nodded, bemused. "What made you think of that?"

"No reason."—But the crinkling sound of his windbreaker brought sudden tears to my eyes; the scent of his drugstore cologne evinced an inexpressible ache.

"Ok then, let's release the emergency brake and get started. Take your time. There's no rush. Want some music?" he asked, opening the glove box in search of his favorite Roger Whittaker tape.

My father's modest car—a blue 1987 Honda Accord— rolled forward, my foot suspended between the brake and gas.

"Try steering," he said. "Get acquainted with the headlights, the windshield wipers. Remember: when you're driving, you're in charge."

He sat uncomfortably in the passenger's seat, long legs cramped against the dash, eyes trained on my hands.

"Grip the wheel tighter. None of this 9 and 3 business. You want your hands at 10 and 2 for maximum control."

As I turned cautious circles around the parking lot, littered with yellow leaves and a smattering of pine cones, my father reminisced about his own father taking him out to the most rural Washington roads, fourteen years old and proudly perched in the front seat of the family pickup truck: first time behind the wheel and already ready to drive his father those long hours home.

"By the time we reached the city, I knew I could drive any-where. It was trial by fire. I was a natural."

I drove to the edge of the pavement bordered by trees, to the place where plastic flowers and a pedestrian walkway marked the end of the parking lot. Here I pushed down on the brake and held my foot steady, feeling the car quiver, then bow to my command.

"What's the matter? Why did you stop?"

I could see it so clearly then—despite the dense curtain of fog, the particular intermittent luxury of the rain: how my father, with each instructive word and glance, placed into my hands the tools of his undoing, of *ours*. Without realizing, he was sculpting the form my leave-taking would take, sketching the map that would guide my exile.

As the ignition turned over, so did our lives: snow globe inside each wheel revolving. As I ventured out into the clean sub-urban streets, flicking my blinker, rehearsing my Washington, my Oregon, my California stops, how I apprenticed myself to his love of motion, the freedom of being carried away. In time, how I would dream it, incessantly: story without commencement or conclusion: creeping home late, stealing my father's car, careen-ing recklessly through a windstorm to Alki Point, then abandon-ing it there—keys skimming lightly across the surface of the waves. *What did I think I was doing? Where did I think I was going?* By the time he found the car, I would be long gone—so long and so far in fact that it sometimes seemed, in dream as in waking, that I had never existed at all.

June 28, 2003. Amarillo, Texas. Lined Paper. Poem. (unsent)

The young men, with their rose-cleft chins, pale whiskers, eyes
enormously opened, remind me always of my father. At my age
now, he had plans to marry, and the woman was a woman I
could not love—and yet I have. For a moment I imagine our
lives converge, hers and mine, in the using of him, the box-
ing of his ears like broken china, shipped ahead of us and
reopened with surprise. The disappointment of it, and our
steady marksmanship, spinning a compass of blame. This
summer, in Amarillo, I found his yellow land where once the
earth nearly swallowed him and the sun freckled his shoulders
in a harried blaze. If he had been then what I am now—cool-
skinned, recalcitrant, with a lazy eye—there is no telling. No
story of big sky and pert green bushes. No terror of sixty, celi-
bate years. For his sake, and theirs, the young men sweating
under white shirts, hungry under brown belts, hurried in their
dark and polished shoes—I wish I had never been born.

Summer 2002. Billings, Montana. 4602 Bruce Avenue.

It was not beautiful—as it should have been. Instead: a rundown
street, a row of ramshackle houses, and a crumbling sidewalk
left without a curb. Children still played in the street the way
my father had recalled. We could hear them hollering through
the alleys as they ran, daring each other to leap over the railroad
tracks: who could jump higher, who farther. I sat calmly in the
car and cemetery-quiet. After all, we had come to visit a grave.

"Wish we had some cigarettes," Angie murmured.

"Seems fitting for this place," I sighed. "Things that burn
up, things that get crushed."

"Things that taste good," she offered.

"That too."

We had passed Billings once before—on our way to Butte and
ever farther westward. We wanted the Coast again, Oregon and
Washington, the jubilance of our bodies in the salty sea air.

Though I had wanted to stop, I chickened the first time, color draining out of my face as we passed the city exits and drove on. Now here we were, back again, days behind: itinerary without a true directive. My grandfather had died before I was born, and my father and I approached a threshold of silence we would not recover from—silence as deep and difficult to accept as death. Those final sentences that no one could commute and no one would forgive.

"Wanna get out? Walk around a little?" Angie suggested.

"No, not really."

We sat in the car across the street from the house like shady characters casing a joint: windows rolled all the way down, silent, staring.

I wanted to smoke too, but I hadn't thought of Marlboro Lights back at the Gulf Station with the man who thought me straight and good, a fine daughter and a future wife. I had basked in his approval as much as I had resented his mistake. *More.* And there was nothing I could do to change that.

"When I was a kid, I could imagine anything," I said. "It was a skill like any other, and I cultivated it well. When my father was away, I conjured him up. I talked to him until I cast his shadow across my bedroom door. I talked to my grandfather and made-believe I heard him answer. Eventually, I heard him without the make-believe. It's possible. Anything is."

I wanted to watch that morning like a slide show against the sky, like movies they show in the park on Sundays. People could bend spoons with their brains. Why couldn't I do this— the ultimate evocation? Picture it, and it's yours. Taste it, and it's melting on your tongue. Smell it, and the world around you reeks of what you dream.

What startled me most I think was the way it was ordinary, the way *they* were: just people who might have been anyone's family but who happened, for no reason at all, to be mine. Aunt Linda, seven years old, playing jacks on the front stoop— her hair yellow as corn, her laugh mustered from deep in her throat. And the door was open, the bright oval window gleaming. My grandmother wore a checkered house dress and open-toed shoes and stood up straighter than I had ever seen her in her arthritic old age. She beat cake batter in a powder-blue bowl, firm but gentle with her ceaseless oscillations. Grandpa John emerged from the house in a short-sleeved, seersucker shirt and pants the color of olives. He heaved a suitcase into the trunk of his car, and his wife and daughter came down to the curb (still standing then) to kiss him good-bye.

"Where's Bill? Has anybody seen him?"

"Probably off playing King of the Mountain," Linda replied.

"Bill! Billy boy!" my grandmother cried. "Your father's off on business. Come say your good-byes!"

"Daddy, can I have a cat?"

"We'll talk about it later, Sweetheart."

"That's what you always say, and it's always later."

"Bill!" John's deep voice now, laced with tobacco.

Angie and I, the never-dreamed-of, the ones who weren't supposed to exist but somehow managed to arrive, lit up our conjured cigarettes, leaned back against our vinyl seats, exhaled. It was memory's longest sigh: menthol and sage and big sky country and *you're gonna burn in hell* and *Jesus loves the little children* and *have a heart, call your mother.*

Around the corner of the modest backyard, a blond-haired boy—with cowlicks and dimples and bright white teeth and sharp blue eyes—came scrambling. He ran fast as he could, and a neighbor dog was tailing him, and another boy shouting, "Wait up, Bill!" I watched as he plunged himself into his father's arms, and John told him, "You might not be king of the mountain, but you're the man of this house while I'm gone," and I winced because I knew better, and I winced again because I knew I didn't really know better, and I thought about my blood and my name and all the hand-me-downs that I would never hand down.

I watched my grandfather driving away, my father chasing

after him and shouting a cheer, and Linda leaning against her mother's apron, wiping her eyes and wondering, *Why does Daddy always have to go away?* And I am chain-smoking again, in my lover's car, burning a hole in the seat with the fiery end of a fifth cigarette. More than an indentation. A kiss to build a dream on. Hands rhubarb-red and cracking open. Just to prove I could.

Summer 2003. Amarillo, Texas. Cracker Barrel Restaurant. I-40 and Quarterhorse Drive.

Our waitress is Jocasta this time. She has an apron with what looks like seventeen stars. I don't have time to count, and Angie turns her eyes to scrape the ground.

"What's going on here? Why are people staring at us?" I whispered.

"Because we're two women who aren't from around here, who aren't traveling with men or wedding rings or cranky babies."

Leaning in close across the table: "Do they *know?*"

"They know enough to know somethin' ain't right, and—"

"And what?"

We ordered corn muffins and grilled chicken tenderloin and that coffee I could never get quite enough of. Jocasta repeated our order word for word, as if daring us to change our minds. When she disappeared into the kitchen, I pleaded again: *"Tell me."*

"Well, you know how when you're trying to be polite—in the North, I mean—you make your letters crisper, you tighten up your speech?" I nodded. "Here—in the South—people tend to think you're mocking them."

"Mocking?"

"Shh! It's ok, but it does make us stand out, even more than we already do."

"I had no idea!"

"I know you didn't. How could you? Welcome to the wonderful world of sore thumbishness, where everything you do is scrutinized and most of what you do misinterpreted."

"So," toying with the peg game, waiting for my warm flush to diffuse, "I guess it's pretty obvious that I don't belong here, huh?"

"*So?* I was raised here—well, not *here*, thank God—but I was raised in the South, and I don't belong either."

"What's going to happen to us?" I ask mournfully.

"Well," unwrapping her silverware with a calm smile and an evenness that soothed me, even there in the public eye, where I couldn't touch her, make my meanings known. "We're going to have lunch, and you're going to soften up your syllables, and we're going to leave Jocasta a generous tip, and then we're going to get in our car and you're going to drive like the speed of light across this state, and the one after, and the one after that."

"Like Thelma and Louise?" I grinned.

"Homoerotic subtext duly noted, but no cliffs please."

It happened just as Angie said it would. We leaned back against the sticky seats of the dust-swabbed Mercury Tracer; she flicked the air conditioner on and hooked the portable CD player into the tape deck so we could hear Patty Griffin sing "Flaming Red" and Emmylou Harris "Red Dirt Girl." *What was it with Southerners and their red?*

"Did I ever tell you how my father was stationed here, with the Air Force, the year before he married my mother?"

"In Amarillo? Really? I didn't know he ever served in the military."

"Oh, yeah. He was almost deployed. They almost sent him to Vietnam."

"My dad was a hippie back then. He said if they'd drafted him, he would have gone to Canada instead."

"I feel like we're fugitives or something."

"Or something," Angie echoed.

"I kinda like it."

"Me too."

I was ready to move on. Another big adventure.

And we passed through the Panhandle without further incident.

Summer 2002. Billings, Montana. Garfield Elementary School. 605 South Billings Boulevard.

Last stop in Yellowstone County: the cyclone gates and rusted swings of my father's first school. Playground painted for hop-scotch and foursquare, pigeons congregating on the jungle gym. We walked toward the long, low building with its dim, fluorescent lights: a few teachers roaming the summer-spare halls. I rang the bell and waited. An uncomfortably pregnant woman wearing a sleeveless dress and crayon-smeared sneakers opened the door and smiled at us without reservation. "What do you need?" she asked warmly.

It was, as usual, a question I came unprepared for. *Why was I there? What explanation could I offer?* Like a child desperate to postpone bedtime, I needed to stall. Haltingly, I told her: "My father was once a student here, and we happened to be passing through the area, and I wondered—"

"Say no more," she replied, waving us in with a careless hand. "Have a look around, what have you. I need to sit down."

We followed inside and stood quietly in the over-air-conditioned corridor. The woman soon disappeared through an adjoining classroom door, and still we stood, aimless, mingling the raised hairs on our sun-soaked arms.

"Happens every time."

"What does?"

"I drop a family-word—something complex like *father*— and all the doors swing wide open."

"You're surprised by this?" Angie began to wander down the hall, tracing the little brown lockers with her open palm. "People respond to what they know."

"But they *don't* know. How can they know if I don't? It's *my* story. He's *my* father."

She shrugged. "They think they know, and that's all that matters."

At the bulletin board, I stopped to browse the first-grade drawings. There seemed to be a *Wizard of Oz* theme in school that year, and the caption construction-papered above these pictures read "No Place Like Home" with a yellow brick border. Children had drawn themselves and their families standing in the front yard of their homes, and on the lines added with sharp-edge to the bottom of each page, the student-artist had printed with wobbly pencil his street address and telephone number.

"Do you see any from Bruce Avenue?"

"No."

"Look closely!" I commanded, scouring the pages for some sign of the newly familiar.

And there it was: not *4602 Bruce Avenue* but a house on the same street with a boy's name boldly scrawled beneath it. Maybe: *Daniel Lawrence lives at 7245 Bruce Avenue with his mom and dad and sister Lucy and cat Pickles.* Or: *My name is Tommy Forester and this is my family. We live in a dark brown house with a big backyard at 5332 Bruce Avenue.* I don't remember the specific inscription, but I do remember the story this particular picture told: two yellow-haired children—a brother pulling his sister in a bright red wagon—a tall, dark-haired mother looking on from the porch, and a tall, dark-haired father standing beside her on the stairs.

"My dad would have drawn a picture like this," I said finally. "It has the look of his reminiscences. Not a lot happening, but the people are happy just the same."

Angie regarded it for a moment. "But *I* would have drawn a picture like that. So would you. The people might look different, but the story would be the same. How a happy family is *supposed* to look. These drawings are as much wishes as they are realities."

———

I stood a long time staring at the drawings, Angie's words buzzing in my ears. "When I was a kid, I thought I was the worst person who ever lived."

"You couldn't have been worse than I was," she sighed.

"Well, turns out I probably *wasn't* the worst person, but I still went around feeling like a criminal all the time."

"Why?"

"This is silly, but—you know that expression *a broken home?*"

"Sure."

"So I heard the phrase, and I learned what it meant, and I wanted it. I *wanted* to come from a broken home."

"Didn't you already?" Then, softening: "I know what you mean, though: the orphan fantasy. I had it, too."

"Not just the Miss Hannigan story and the British nanny fantasy and the whole Brady Bunch blended family dream. It was more than that. There was something *specific* I wanted. Not always, but often. I thought about it. I hated myself for it. I wanted my mother"—turning back to study the wall—"*out of the picture.*"

"And she knew?"

"*Knew?* She was the one who put the idea into my head, then turned around and tortured me for even *thinking* of it."

The pregnant woman had returned, sipping a Snapple and pressing the cold bottle between her collar bones. "How's everything? You two doing all right?"

I nodded. "In fact, we were just leaving. You don't mind if we take a couple pictures on our way out?"

Of this rather unremarkable roll of film, there is one picture I hold dear. It's of Angie and me, leaning against a brick wall under a sign that reads *Garfield School.* The teacher, sensing my desire to commemorate something, perhaps sensing also that I didn't quite know how, offered to take a picture of the two of us.

"Your father—is he still living?"

"Yes."

"Well then, I'm sure he would want a picture of his daughters, here where it all began." She was kind, and we didn't have the heart to tell her. And we had, after all, made this pilgrimage together.

Our eyes met then, as the camera flashed, as the woman waved us on like children dawdling after curfew: *you girls get on home now!* All at once we burst into laughter.

Epilogue

June 8, 2005. Orlando, Florida. Radisson Resort. Hotel Stationery. (unsent)

> *Dear Dad, I was thinking of you tonight as I rented a car at the airport, driving out in the Florida dusk — a stranger to this city, its toll roads and traffic. You were right, though, about this state — the palm trees are spectacular, and the night air sweet as perfume. I remember you came here on business once, met with clients for drinks and steaks by the pool. You couldn't stop talking about that pool: how it sparkled, the waterfalls and landscaping like a natural lagoon.*

> *I'm proud to report I've become a superb driver, thanks in no small part to you. People feel safe when they ride with me, the way I used to feel safe with you. I remember curling up in the back seat and sleeping through long car rides — peaceful, unbroken sleep — trusting you would bring us safely home through any dark. In that respect, you never let me down.*

> *I came to Orlando for a conference. I was asked to come and give a reading of some of my poems. That's tomorrow, though, and this is tonight, and I'm thinking of you and the long years that have passed since last we saw each other — longer still since I've heard your voice on the phone, your hearty humble laugh. I just miss you, Dad, that's all. My life must*

seem so foreign to you now. I live in a city whose skyline you wouldn't recognize; I eat foods you wouldn't even try. "Soy," you'd say—"like the sauce?" And yes, I still love the woman I loved the last time we talked, in case you're wondering, which you probably are. We have a house with a porch and a yard and two fat cats who keep our laps warm, even in the coldest weather.

I have this recurring dream. I've had it for a long time, but it's not like the nightmares, which have mostly stopped now—perhaps (I'm hoping) for good. I dream about our reunion, and when we meet, it's somewhere tropical, like here. I told Angie I thought it was Miami, but in a pinch, Orlando will do. Anyway, remember how you always used to say if I studied hard and gave my all, I'd be able to "write my own ticket someday"? Well, I never knew what you were talking about, what that saying really meant to convey. Just another aphorism, another pebble skimming the waves. But I know how you love golf, and I know how Mom never lets you play. When was the last time you saw the green, Dad? When was the last time you held those golden clubs in your hands and made a long, smooth drive down the fairway? Not since I've been alive, and you've been reminiscing about it longer.

Florida is rife with golf courses, Dad. It's full of air-conditioned retirement homes and widows who'd bake you casseroles and play cribbage all day. Maybe that's overstepping, but there'd be friends too, and plenty of penny ante poker and Jimmy Stewart westerns and golfing till you ran out of polo shirts and goofy plaid. And I would visit and caddy for you, Dad. Remember: the way you always wanted me to? The way you always said we would?

In the dream, I write my own ticket, and it's for you. One-way from Seattle to Miami, though if you want, we can make it a train ticket to Montana, and you can catch a plane from there. I know Mom hasn't been kind to you either, and when I left for good, maybe I felt some small streak of vengeance— now he'll have to live with it, live with her. I may have thought this then, but I didn't mean to punish you. I still want for your happiness the way I still try to believe you want for mine.

Take the ticket. Have a heart. Do yourself a favor. Is that the feeling now, of all your own advice come back to haunt you? Well, here's something you never said: wherever this letter finds you, whatever the time of day, drop whatever it is you're doing. Stop mid-sentence. Don't bother with the suitcase or the garment bag. This is me urging you forward, on with your life: "Be brave, Dad!" Just get into your car and drive.

Triptych of My Father, George Bailey in Another Life

First Panel

Montana cold is its own cross to bear. Be it Butte or Billings where, like Bedford Falls, the boy learns early about thin ice — skating or sledding, skidding through to unexpected places. *No harm done*, he says, hoisting himself over the ledge, tracing his own tracks back through the blizzard. His father, gone much of the month, sells tires for Goodyear; his mother cooks beef stew and sips coffee piping hot from the pot. His sister is fragile, stays mostly indoors. In the spring, he'll bring her rocks and worms.

Then, they move west, where the snow becomes rain, the whiteouts replaced by torrents and gales. Instead of a malt shop, he gets a job mowing lawns, takes a paper route that has him up before dawn. An ambitious boy: gold cowlicks of an impish Jay North, determined curiosity of a Frank or Joe Hardy. Once, he wished a teacher cheerfully, "Merry Christmas — and happy hangover!" believing the phrase referred to the days that *hang over* after Christmas, an extension of his favorite holiday. Once, he saved all the dandelions from a neighbor's front lawn and placed them proudly on her porch in a vase. "But they're weeds, honey," his mother explained when the woman came outside, clutching her robe and cursing. "Who says?" he demanded, indignant. "I think, if it looks like a flower, it is."

The girls always like Bill Wade. He is clean-cut and courteous, the Dobie Gillis of Denny Middle School and later, of Chief Sealth High. He carries the books for many a Mary, offers a ride to many a Violet—in the car he saved up for, that shiny red roadster with chrome running boards and bench seats sheathed in white leather. Sunday mornings his father watches from his chair, smoking a dark pipe and smiling. *Attaboy, son,* as he scours the tires with an SOS pad, as he wipes dry the glistening hood with a chamois. Maybe the father knows he is fated to die young, his own life a precarious sled on the ice, careening suddenly out of control. He consoles himself that Bill can tie a slipknot like the best of them and shine the hell out of a pair of shoes. He has a dimple in his left cheek *for wooing the ladies,* but a handshake that conveys *he's all man.* Now the son stands tall and straight in his church coat, a string-bean body in a broad man's clothes—lithe as Dick Van Dyke, moon-faced as Jimmy Stewart—the suitcase of his heart stuffed to brimming, and a coarse, taut lasso in his hand.

Second Panel

In this story, there is no broken-down Building and Loan, no Granville House with gutters spilling and piano trilling out of tune. Nothing second-rate or second-hand. On the icy surface of their lives, everything looks right, and Bill commends himself and his new wife: "I think, if it looks right, it is." She couldn't agree more. Recall the story you think you know—two girls vying for the heart of one boy, who becomes the man who proclaims, "I don't want to get married, *ever,* to *anyone,* do you understand? I want to do what *I* want to do!" In this story, there is no binary between "the bachelor" and "the family man," no fine line drawn between the "Donna Reed type" and the "Gloria Grahame." Bill Wade was made to settle down, and where matrimony is a foregone conclusion, the question becomes not *if*, not *when*, but *whom*. Recall the story you think you know—Potter's proposal, which Bailey turns down; the speech, rendered from his quivering lips, his hand waving the hardly-smoked cigar: "In the whole vast configuration of things, I'd say you were nothing but a scurvy little spider." Welcome to the web, Bill. In the story behind the story, watch yourself carry your nemesis across the threshold. Marriage was always a metaphor, and Potter was always vehicle to your tenor, bringing you back to yourself like the face in the mirror, cut shaving again, then dotted with little white lies. All the better for sopping up blood.

When the daughter comes, she is made in the father's image, not the mother's. This slight will kindle a new contention between them. As when she is walking home from school in a rainstorm, the broad coat unbuttoned and swinging loose on her string-bean body, a bouquet of dandelions clasped tightly in her hand. "Those are weeds, you know," the mother reprimands, but the daughter's illusion is not shattered. She understands that nomenclature is less powerful than perception, yet—and this is the part that troubles her father—perception isn't everything either. "Should we put those flowers in a glass?" he asks, gesturing toward the bedside table. Forget the story you thought you knew. Zuzu shakes her Shirley Temple curls, chanting, "Mama had a baby and its head popped off," gold crowns everywhere severed from stems. The father disapproves, and the daughter consoles him: "Don't worry, Daddy. It isn't literal." For such a twist as this, the father has no context.

Third Panel

For every journey, there is a Darkest Night. Call it the climax. Call it the katabasis. It's an Everyman story, so you should call it whatever you like. George Bailey hurtles headlong into the furious waves, determined to end his life or save another's. (Could these be compatible fates?) But for Bill Wade, there can

be no contemplation of a death, for such would require contemplation of a life—*his* life—all the mornings, evenings, and
afternoons, measured out in silver spoons and well-varnished
religion, stocks and bonds. Now, approaching the fulcrum of
middle age, he finds himself—part Prufrock, part Goodman
Brown, the Kafkaesque and Capraesque combine—entwined
in the same web he once spun for the woman he loved. Their
whole, vast configuration of things. And things. And things.
The daughter, one of these things, what Potter would call their
capital, then turn a comb to her recalcitrant curls.

On this Darkest Night, Potter empties Bailey's pockets. He
has been spending quarters on coffee, tipping too well, beef
jerky at the gas station and chocolate bars at the mall. The
total debit is small—*negligible*—but they didn't get ahead that
way. Pennies were made for pinching, not tossing in a wishing
well, not *wasting*. She'll have to let out his trousers again. *Is
that flesh there*—driving a sharp fist to his gut, twisting till he
coils in pain—*or are you practicing to play Santa Claus next
year?* Potter likes to tell the story of the string bean she smashed
to succotash, how he had really *packed on the pounds* while
she scrimped and starved, *slim and trim* as the day they were
married.

Bill Wade, who is a praying man, folds his weary hands and
bows his silver head, recites their blessings. *No harm done*, he
says, for if it looks like a family, it surely is. Then, he turns out
the porch light, and a thick fog settles over the stars. They sleep
like soldiers in the trench of their bed, bodies rigid, brows per-
petually bent. In dreams, she'll return the coins to his pocket,
rescind his charge, while he hunches away, hungry again, to
the inviolable pantry of R.E.M. Visions of sugar plums, a clock
chiming "Auld Lang Syne"; in the distance, a barely audible
bell. In this story, there is a quilt dotted with dandelions, a pile
of heads and a pile of tails. In this story, nothing is literal, and
everything is. *Let's flip for it*. A daughter weeps softly, wishes
she had never been born.

The Flower of Afterthought

I end not far from my going forth
By picking the faded blue
Of the last remaining aster flower
To carry again to you.
　　　　　—Robert Frost, "A Late Walk"

The only story I knew about estrangement was the Parable of the Prodigal Son. There had been no primer, no *Child's Guide to Becoming Lost*—only hearsay, and heresy, and the bricked-up chimney of the heart.

In the first place, I was not a son. I was intended to surrender my name, to part with my inheritance and accept my husband's fortune—be it good, or be it lacking. I was not a wife, nor would I be, which meant my disobedience extended far into the future. Without grandchildren, my parents had nothing left to hope for. I had denied them their passport to posterity. What reason had they to kill a fatted calf?

I was also the only child, so my elder brother did not stand in the fields wringing his hands, did not envy me the extravagant welcome awaiting my return. If there was to be a homecoming, I understood it would take place on their terms. I knew how I would be handled, how suspiciously and decisively appraised: the kid gloves, the white van. . . .

Perhaps our misunderstanding began with the word *prodigal* itself. In recounting this parable, my parents had explained

151

that prodigal meant *wrong* or *sinful*. It was the story of the Bad Son, the Morally Corrupt Son, they told me. Years later, when I reached for the word, a teacher suggested I might mean *rebel* or *visionary*. "You see, to be prodigal is not necessarily to be delinquent," she explained. "It can also mean generous to a fault, one who spares nothing."

It has been nine years now. I know what it is to carry the terrible weight of *thus* and *therefore*, two ballasts bent in equal parts despair. No explanation, only outcome. I am to my family what earthquakes are to waves: conspicuous disruption of continuity, of certainty. I happened beneath their surface, below their radar. I began with a tremor and culminated in a devastation. After hashish and Hail Mary; after rock salt and studded tires; after insufficient postage and reckless penmanship—accusations lodged inside apologies—after so much *weathering* that I have forgotten who, in fact, is the storm: my surrender takes new form.

Prologue

"Are you feeling any better today?" Dr. Weise inquires. He is always calm, with his palms face down on his knees in what seems an alternative posture to prayer.

"Much," I reply, taking a tentative seat on the chair. "I've made a decision."

"Tell me about it," he says.

By the soft light of this office, I have studied my past, unfolded the furrowed blueprints of my childhood, adolescence, and beyond: my coming out, my coming of age, my final comings and goings from a place I never belonged but for which I seem always to be longing. I have listened to his insistent credo, week after week, year after year: *You did what you had to do. You told the truth. You saved yourself. Be at peace now with the woman you love and with the woman you are.*

"I want to thank you for all your patience and compassion.

I know you listened, and I believe you heard everything I said and advised me the best you were able."

Dr. Weise has placed (strategically, I imagine, although I never asked) a mirror on the far side of the room, so when a disclosure becomes difficult and the impulse is to look away, the person in my position is forced to meet her own eyes. So I rise now, and I face the mirror, and I see Dr. Weise stoically positioned in his chair (the background), and my own expressive features (the foreground), and I notice again the proliferation of gray around my temples and streaking my forehead like a recalcitrant wave. My father turned silver by thirty; "prematurely," he'd say. And that was, symbolically, the reason I stood here today: to refute that birthright, not to have it redeemed; to sever us, once and for all.

"This will be my last session," I announce.

"I see," Dr. Weise replies, visibly surprised. "May I ask why?"

"It has to do with Kant."

"The philosopher?"

"Yes, the *moral* philosopher. It occurred to me that I like the concept of parables because they offer a moral, not in the strict ethical sense, but—something to learn from, to abide by. A message of some kind. In all this business of estrangement, I've been desperate for a guideline."

"So you've taken up philosophy?"

"Only casually. But I remembered Kant from college, how austere he seemed and how absolutely committed to being a good man and to making the rubric for goodness available to others with his categorical imperative."

"Refresh my memory," says Dr. Weise.

"Well, it's pretty accessible for eighteenth-century prose. It might make a nice bumper sticker or framed crochet: *Act only according to that maxim whereby you can at the same time will that it should become a universal law.*"

"And how does this imperative apply to your feelings about your family?"

"I think—and I don't want to hurt you by saying this—" I turn from the mirror and move back toward the center of the room—"that you and Kant are invested in entirely different methods of goodness. In a nutshell, I think you're a consequentialist, and you counsel from that perspective."

Dr. Weise laces his fingers now, draws a deep breath, exhales. "I'm noticing—not judging but noticing—that you're intellectualizing again. You tend to put ideas into high-order categories when you need to feel you have control over them—over yourself."

"Or maybe that's just how I make sense of the world. When I don't have enough of my own words anymore, I start looking for others. You gave me some. I stopped seeing myself as a *fugitive* and began calling myself a *survivor*. You distinguished between *forced exile* and *deliberate choices*, my freedom to choose my own path even if it meant transgressing my parents' wishes. Which it did mean. Which it still means. But I don't want to continue on this path. You've presented your case. You've convinced me that plenty of adult children end contact with *destructive family members*, leave behind *toxic domestic environments*. What is it you always say? *Peace replaces guilt*. I'm supposed to let go of this guilt. I'm supposed to walk to the end of the plank with all my guilt in a burlap bag—and the bag's weighted with rocks, of course, so it can never resurface—and instead of plunging my own body overboard, I repeat some mantra—*It wasn't to hurt them; it was to honor myself*—and drop my burden into the sea. *Peace replaces guilt*. Only it doesn't. Not for me."

"We have more work to do," he suggests. I admire his capacity for gentle rigor. "Peace is a process. You learn peace over time—the way you learned guilt, even if you don't remember learning it."

"What I was saying before, about you being a consequentialist—that wasn't an insult. It only means you take a more personal view of the world. And sometimes you might be willing to rationalize certain actions because they result in what appears to be progress, something *better* than what came before."

"You're talking about ends and means here, and that's fine, but let's be clear, Julie: you had every right and every reason to liberate yourself from an *oppressive family structure.* Can you honestly tell me you aren't happier now than you were before?"

"But that's personal. I'm happier in my daily life, but the guilt lingers, and I think it's supposed to linger, because it's not just a personal matter. Kant believed in a Bigger Picture, a notion of moral duty that could be generalized. Surely estrangement is not desirable as a universal law. Who will take care of my parents when they're old? How will I live with myself and with all the—" reaching for the word again—"all the *prodigal* silence after they're gone?"

For the first time, a frantic look comes over his face. "You're not thinking of going back, are you?"

"Oh, Dr. Weise. I'm *always* thinking of going back, but that's not the answer. It would only make me miserable, and it would never really make them happy. They grieve because they know they had a daughter and they lost her, which I imagine is quite a different feeling than when they thought they could never have children at all. That loss could never be comparable to this one, and I of course never asked to be born."

"Julie, we've discussed the George Bailey fantasy at length—"

I hold up my hand. "It's what I've chosen. This is the only way to maximize our common good. We all know I've failed as a daughter. Forget fault; forget pointing the compass of blame. I don't want to suffer knowing that my parents suffer. I can live with anything I've chosen as long as they never have to know that they are the ones who *weren't* chosen."

"So what do you propose to do exactly?"

"It's done. I can't tell you how, but I'm free of this now. I have my memory of a history that never took place, and my family has no memory of it. In their world, we are not estranged; I simply do not exist. So we can go on now, in the best way for all of us—as strangers whose lives need never intersect."

Dr. Weise wanted to reach for his phone. He wanted to have me taken in for observation. He considered in the quiet of his own mind whether these might be the fabled "psychotic features" of the agitated depression from which he always believed I suffered and for which I had persistently refused medication. *Talking should be enough*, I said. Now I was tired of talking, tired of wondering what my parents were doing, how they were coping, the new lies they created to account for my absence.

Indulging me this last time, Dr. Weise takes a different approach. "You know, George Bailey wasn't happy with his unborn life."

"Well, how could he be? He didn't choose it."

"But in a way he did. He *wished* for it. His wish must have been very sincere. Isn't the moral of that story that not being born becomes its own kind of burden?"

I am standing by the door. I am studying the room with the scruples of a student before final exams. "We are parallel lines now," I tell him, meaning all of us—he, my parents, me. And as is fitting to mark the end of our intersection, I race down the stairs of the building and out into the street, where it is snowing like the night everything changed for George Bailey. The people have a nostalgic way about them, wrapping scarves over their heads as they duck under awnings and into coffeehouses. Then, the snow ceases, and the steeped aroma of spring thickens through the trees, and this too is what I have wished for.

Parable in Which I Encounter My Mother Among the Perishable Goods

On the night before Thanksgiving, I have gone to the grocery in pursuit of canned cranberries and boxed stuffing. With no need for a decadent affair, Angie and I have agreed to deli-sliced turkey sandwiches and a festival of horror films.

This is the way it happens—as it must—when I see my mother (aging, daughterless) standing before me in the aisle. We are occupants of the same city again, and we will pass each other here, as elsewhere, with the same, slightly guarded indifference. I feel my temperature rise, an unexpected longing as our carts nearly collide. Without meeting my eyes, she murmurs, "I beg your pardon."

Now *pardon* is another word that bends and burns with meaning. I had wanted, more than anything, to be pardoned, for my mother to turn to me and pronounce an unthinkable decree: "Yes, dear, I was impossible to live with. Yes, darling, you deserve to be free of me." Linda, my mother, was no stranger to this yearning. She had been cast the black sheep of a devoutly white family, shunted from pasture to pasture by her mother's cold shoulder, her father's fickle tongue: harsh words and harsher silence. She would have done anything to please them, to transform apathy and reprimand—oscillating tersely—to some gentle acknowledgment of her presence, let alone to praise. I recall her stories: late nights working at the Sears store downtown, riding the bus home in darkness, scurrying past the deserted storefronts of the West Seattle Junction—more than a mile through that pin-drop night where every stray sound or shadow stretched her imagination to terror. Each Friday she brought daffodils from Pike Place Market, and each Friday her mother shrugged, took them grudgingly, shoved the bright stems into a second-hand vase on a counter out of sight of the sun.

When her brother announced his engagement, my young parents—just newlyweds themselves—did not receive the news. A party was given in Steve's honor. The brother and his fiancée were lavished with gifts and entertainment: a ballroom rented out, an orchestra commissioned. It was a nosy aunt who called my mother, inquiring whether she had been ill, wondering what had kept her away. "I couldn't get a straight answer from your mother, so I thought I'd ask you myself."

Linda called home, desperate for an explanation. "We thought you'd be too busy with your teaching," her mother had said. "We weren't sure you and Bill would have anything nice to wear." Unabashed, she told her oldest daughter: "They just wanted a small affair. You'll come to the wedding. We'll be able to accommodate you there."

And so commenced another silence, which my mother had chosen, even against her will. She did not attend the wedding; she did not return the calls. She could not be coaxed out of hiding, despite their apathy or their reprimand or even her own curiosity, by which she was often consumed.

"When did you start talking to Grandma again?" I asked her once. We sat on my mother's bed as she painted our fingernails—mine first, then hers; all the while, a salty sea breeze rustled the curtains.

"When you were born," she said. "Your father called my mother from the hospital. He thought it was the right thing to do."

"And what did you think?" I studied her for the first time as a creature apart, a woman alone. Something about the way she curled her fingers and blew on her nails, eyes downcast, poignant as a lost child. Was this how my father had felt, saddened by her sadness, wanting only to save her?

"It had been seven years. I didn't know the right thing anymore. I couldn't imagine. But she had been cruel to me, unspeakably cruel—" It was then that my mother met my eyes. "We spoke then because I knew I didn't need her anymore."

"How did you know?"

Tightening her hold on my hand: "Because I had you."

Linda has passed me now, passed without properly seeing. I am half-disappointed that she won't recognize me; the other half is palpably relieved. I follow her through the store, tempting our fate, tempting her to turn around and confront me for standing too close, for sifting through her shopping cart, for staring. In line behind her at the checkout, I watch as she sorts her coupons, signs her name, declines accompaniment to the car.

But she leaves her checkbook, and the clerk calls after her but she doesn't hear, so I leave my basket and spring into action, disturbing the stillness of that pin-drop night, the parking lot mostly deserted, potholed and puddled.

"Wait!" I shout, and she turns from the trunk of the car, placing her cart between us as a barricade. Her face is full of fear which, on closer inspection, seems always to have been there, even in my memories of her and in the photographs I once had ransomed—which since then have eerily begun to disappear.

"Don't hurt me," comes her quivering command.

"No, ma'am." The word is soft on my tongue like melting snow, the vowel oscillating between what it had been and what it has become. *Ma'am* now, nothing more. I hold out the leather book engraved with her initials—LMW—the middle and last of which are also mine. "You left this behind. In there. Just now." I am out of breath and trembling, holding tight to the cliff of her eyes. "I'm sorry if I scared you."

Our hands touch in passing. She does not trust me. She never has. And her nails are as white and bare as the cleft moon rising, over her shoulder, through the fractured air.

Parable in Which I Encounter My Father Beside the Duamish River

The first time was an accident; the second could not be so. I had seen her, and now I wanted to see him.

"Do we have any bread?" I ask my beloved across the kitchen table.

"You've had three pieces and almost all of the jam."

"Stale, I mean—something I could feed the birds."

Angie appraises me, bewildered. "What birds are you feeding?"

"At the park." I try to sound casual. "I'm going for a walk today."

"Do you want some company?"

"No, no. I have a story I'm thinking through. I won't be gone long, but I need to go alone."

"It's cold," Angie observes. "Take a windbreaker."

I remember these roads so well, the way my father drove to work every morning before the sun took its place in the sky, when most of the city lights were merely flashing, commanding only caution, nothing as final as stop or go.

If my hunch was right, Bill Wade still walked by the water. I had stopped believing some time ago that he could walk *on* it, but this too was a parable with which I struggled to part. We used to walk together—at Alki Beach or Lincoln Park or around our neighborhood—and over the years, our conversations came to center on my mother.

"She used to be happy, I think—I *thought*. Her family situation wasn't ideal, but we prayed about it, and the wounds seemed to heal."

"Do you think a person can ever feel the same after losing so much? It has to be different now—but maybe not different enough."

"I've given her a good life, you know. She has the house she always wanted, the garden of her dreams. She's surrounded every day by beautiful things. And you—you just mean the world to your mother. You were the thing she wanted most of all, the thing she feared she'd never have."

"There's a lot of pressure involved in being wanted so much," I'd tell him softly. "Sometimes I don't think I could ever be enough."

"You shouldn't blame yourself. I guess I've never been able to please her, but I'll be damned if I know why."

So I learned my father too felt guilty, imagined he had failed. Like me, he sensed that something was deeply, perhaps inexpressibly wrong. Yet as we strolled the long promenade between the rocky beach and the storm-tossed trees, he began to rescind this story, closing in on himself and turning away from me. I watched, like a ship at sea, the progressive capsize of his conviction that something was not as it ought to be.

"Just what do you mean by that?" he'd ask, suddenly defensive.

"Well, there's the screaming, and the slamming doors, and the threats she makes, and the devastating things she says—"

"She doesn't mean them, Julie. That's what you've got to understand about your mother. She might have a shorter fuse than we'd like, but—"

"Dad." I'd touch his arm, stop him in his tracks. "We're not talking about a few words said in anger. We're talking about rage—an all-consuming rage."

"It's not rage exactly. She gets upset sometimes, but *rage*? That's going too far."

"Is reading our mail going too far? Is not permitting any door in the house to be closed or any phone call to be taken in private going too far?"

"Jesus, Julie, you make it sound like you're living under house arrest!"

Then, I'd let my silence speak for me. I'd watch as my father fed bread to the birds, the sea gulls and mallards and even the crows that had not been invited but had a way of infringing on these impromptu feasts. When the bag was empty, my father would wrap his arm around my shoulder and remind me what a good life we had; how sometimes I overreacted, which was only natural, being a teenaged girl. Still, I should learn to have patience with my mother, who loved me more than life itself, even if she didn't always know the best way to show it.

"Because at the end of the day, you couldn't ask for a better mother, and I couldn't ask for a better wife. So what are we doing here?" he'd say, resolved. "Let's make like a family. Let's go home."

Today I find my father outside the building where he works, on his lunch hour, roaming a man-made path beside the Duamish River. We had never walked here together before, but I knew he craved the solitude, and I remembered how he spoke of these Canada geese and their fondness for his sandwich-crusts, which he almost always saved.

Bill Wade, who is no longer a young man, still carries the hopefulness of youth about him. He has a light step and a reassuring smile, and despite his most persistent combing, a cowlick still sprouts from the crest of his head.

"Hello," I say, knowing it will not be hard to strike up a conversation. What is difficult instead is to gaze into his pale blue eyes without wincing, without letting on I know more than I should.

"Beautiful day, isn't it?" he replies.

"Sure is."

"I've never minded a little winter chill. Makes the air seem twice as fresh—that's what I always say."

I nod and withdraw my prop from my pocket: a Ziploc bag brimming with scraps of bread.

"You're a bird-feeder, too, I see," and his face beams—this approval I have always sought.

"You work for Boeing, I take it?"

"Twenty years this April," he smiles. "Had a long career in sales before I took this job. Went out at the top of my game." Bill Wade takes his hands from his pockets, rubs them together for warmth. "What about you? Are you an engineer in training?"

"No, no—I write. I'm a writer."

"For a newspaper?" he asks.

"No. Mostly for myself, I guess."

"Like a novelist? My wife likes that Danielle Steel."

"Sort of," I smile. "I'm not quite as successful as Danielle Steel." Then, to clarify: "I have a day job."

"Well, would I know anything you've written then?" He is genuinely curious, genuinely kind.

"Probably not," I reply, blushing, then open my bag for the birds.

Awhile later, we have stopped walking and stand together in silence, several feet apart, as the geese crowd around us, cautiously grateful. Such is my own feeling, here in the presence of my former father, who will not now even imagine my name.

"I don't guess I've ever known a real writer," he remarks. "When I retire, I'd like to read more, maybe even take up writing myself. My sister liked to write some when she was a child, but I think she's all but given that up now."

"How is your sister?" I ask without thinking, and he begins to reply, only to pause mid-sentence and consider my face more closely.

"I'm sorry. It's just that—have we met before?"

"Maybe. I come here sometimes—to walk or to write. I don't live terribly far, and"—with a deep sigh—"you too seem familiar somehow."

His face relaxes again, but he does not tell me about my aunt or my mother or any more at all about his life. Instead, he sits down on a nearby bench, laces his hands behind his head, and begins to whistle. I am not sure if this is his way of conveying that our conversation has ended, that he prefers to be alone now with the scenery and with his own thoughts on this chilly December day.

As I am about to move on, he calls after me: "Where can I find something you've written? The Walden Books at the mall?"

"No," shaking my head. "I'm not so commercial as all that. But the next time I see you"—a promise now—"I'll bring something I've written to share."

Bill Wade stretches his long legs, leans back against the wood of this chosen pew. "Deal," he says. His whistling continues after me, trite and sweet as a music box slowly winding down.

Parable in Which I, a Story Teller, Encounter My Mother, a Bank Teller

We are standing face to face with a sheet of glass between us. In this respect, nothing has changed. She wears a badge with raised gold letters pinned to her blazer's lapel. I carry a driver's license in my tattered green bag.

"May I help you?" Linda asks, and as she lifts her eyes to meet mine through the bandit barrier—a solid inch of bullet-proof glass—I look down again; I turn, ever so slightly, away.

Of course I could have chosen any bank in the city to open my account. Our meeting is not accidental this time, nor is it truly benign. I have come here with a question, an experiment, in mind.

My mother left teaching the year I was twelve, the same year her own mother died. She had wanted to prove to all who were watching that she was a faithful child, driving forty miles each way each day to sit at her mother's side—to reclaim those vanquished good graces that in fact had never been hers to misplace.

Heavily drugged and only marginally conscious, her mother had mostly forgotten the fact of her children; their faces blurred one and the same. She thought Linda alternately a nurse or an angel, though sometimes a bandit who had stolen her purse and her clothes, leaving only the unfashionable hospital robe. "You're a sly one," she'd murmur, one eye wide. "Where have you taken my treasures?"

My mother never knew what her mother remembered, even less what her mother forgave. She was not thinking then of her own rage, only of the sorrow—ever unfinished—that eclipsed the source of her pain. In this respect, my mother and I were the same. We had lost the women we came from, and this burden blemished us, though perhaps in different ways.

When she went back to her old school, my mother found the position there had been taken. She looked for work and found only this job, a bank clerk at a branch on the "bad side" of town. No matter. She would work her way up, a new project to throw herself into. I watched her leave the house in her best business suit, hair teased and sprayed, lips and nails painted to match. "We don't need the money," my father had said. "Why are you putting yourself through this?" But I understood. I understood better than anyone that longing to step outside myself and into another room, a waiting role. My mother had always been quick with numbers, had always enjoyed the heft of a deck of cards or a stack of bills, sifting them through her fidget-prone fingers.

This year—the year of the bank, the year of my mother's orphaning and my own body's sudden betrayal—was also the year of Scott. Scott had transferred to my mother's branch as an assistant manager, the person to whom she would directly report. He was a soft-spoken man with a house in Queen Anne and a husband (yes, *husband*) who played in a rock-and-roll band. When I came to meet my mother at the end of her shift or for a lunch break on Saturday afternoons, I would stand in the corner near her supervisor's desk, studying the snapshot of Scott and David in their wedding best. This picture of two men, tuxedo-clad and smiling, clasping each other on the steps of a church or museum—I wasn't sure which—filled me to bursting with a frightened desire and also, an inexplicable joy.

Scott was kind to my mother. They got along well. She always spoke of him fondly. "And the Other Thing—" she had told me, leaning in across the table, her stout voice shrinking suddenly lean: "That's *his* mother's hardship, not mine."

"Who says it's a hardship?" I mustered. "Wouldn't you love me as much if I were—"

Then, her eyes blazed. Then, the glass between us reflected back to us the stage lights of our impossible story. "Never finish that sentence—" her icy command. "If you want to kill me, take this knife now, and let's be done."

Sentence is another word that bends and burns with meaning. She was speaking of a string of syllables that satisfy the grammatical rules of a language. I was thinking of a conviction under criminal law and the prison term to accompany it. I thought how, already, in my tinder heart, I flamed with hypothetical love. There would come a choice then—between my mother's contempt and my lover's consent—between two open vaults of honest knowing: *family* or *family*. Enter the first wish of our undoing:

"So if I weren't your daughter—" I pressed.

"But you *are* my daughter."
"But if I *weren't*—"
"*But you are.*"

The woman, who is not my mother any longer, does not recognize me from the supermarket, least of all from my other
life. "May I help you?" she says again, and I respond, cautiously grateful.

"Yes. I'd like to open a savings account."

"Do you have any other accounts with this bank?"

"No. My partner and I have a joint checking account with
Washington Mutual, but I wanted to open a private account to
put some money away for her birthday."

This time Linda is the one who looks down. "I see," comes
her late reply. "You'll need to fill out these forms." I watch her
pale hand passing them through the scooped silver tray.

If Angie were here, she'd say I was writing this prophesy
toward its own fulfillment. She'd ask with concern: "Why give
her this chance to hurt you again?"

If Angie were here, she'd be right, of course, but I still
favored the lie. I chose to believe I had come here, not for
indictment, but instead for exoneration. *Be different this time.*
Please, Mom, be different this time.

"You see," I tell Linda Wade, "it's been a hard year for me.
I lost my parents this year, and—though we were never close,
I've felt lonelier now, knowing the loss is final."

"Oh," she murmurs. "I'm sorry." I hear in her voice a qua-
ver of compassion. She raises her head, returning my gaze.

I trace my fingers along the tiny beads chaining this pen
to the glass. "Angie, my partner, has made all the difference.
Without her, I don't know how I would have gotten along."

Linda clears her throat. I have made her uncomfortable.
She is torn now between empathy and exprobation. "If you'd
step aside please, I'll help the next customer. Come back to the
window when you're done."

———

As I transpose my life into these lines and boxes, I notice a man pass through the corridor behind the teller cages. He wears a dark shirt and a striking blue tie with a key wrapped around his wrist on a coil. I recognize him at once from his picture and from the past, which is also a kind of picture, superimposed over all those still frames of wanting and would-have-beens.

Linda catches his eye. He smiles. They exchange a signal of some kind. Without question, Scott steps forward and waves me toward a vacant window.

"How may I help you today?"

"I'm here to open a savings account. *She* was helping me—" gesturing to my mother as she counts a stranger's change. "I'm in no rush. I don't mind waiting."

"Linda's overdue for a break," he replies. "I'd be happy to assist you here."

In the periphery, she concludes her transaction. She locks her money drawer, straightens her skirt, withdraws her key. "Now I'll just need two pieces of identification," Scott instructs. Absently, I pass him my driver's license. Linda glances toward us, then quickly away.

"And your second piece of identification?"

"Oh—I'm sorry. What would that be?"

"A passport—do you have a passport?" I shake my head. "Well, a birth certificate then?"

"Of course." I reach into my bag, the zippered side pocket where I keep such things. I can hear Linda's heels crossing the tile. In a moment, she will disappear all together from view. "I've always kept it right here . . ." I say, fumbling through the pay stubs and newspaper clippings. Then, the fumbling stops, and a wave of pure cold passes through my body. My hand cramps. My heart thuds. I see it all so clearly, like the first moment after a dream: *Zuzu's petals.*

"Ma'am?"

"I'm sorry. I don't have it. I thought I did, but it's gone."

"Is it possible to ask your parents for a copy?"

"No, I'm afraid it isn't."

"Well, perhaps if you contact the hospital where you were born—"

But of course the hospital has no such records. Scott encourages me to come back with the proper credentials. He regards me kindly, yet I sense the suspicion under his eyes. He will leave me now and proceed to the break room where my mother is heating her microwave dinner, peeling her overripe orange. She will be coy and tell him only, "There was just something strange about her. I had a gut feeling. I hope you didn't mind." And Scott will pat her hand and promise, "Not to worry, my dear. Not any trouble at all."

Then, thinking of it, deliberating a moment before he declares: "That customer back there—the odd one—"

"Yes?" Her eyebrows arch in anticipation.

"It's a funny thing, but I noticed she had your last name."

Parable in Which the Newspaper Gives Me Away

Picture this: a Saturday in spring, the lilac bushes battering our windows, their fragrance seeping through the screen door.

"You've been awfully quiet this morning," Angie notes, parsing the *Times* into piles.

"I'm just restless, that's all. I didn't sleep very well last night."

"Something on your mind?"

"No . . . I don't think so. Should I make a French press?"

Her mouth widening into smile: "Yes please!"

In the kitchen, I fill the kettle. I grind the beans. I lift the phone and listen for messages. Then, Angie calls from the living room: "What do you know about your birth flower?"

"My birth flower?"

"There's a silly little write-up about them in the paper. May is lily of the valley, and September is—"

"The aster," I say, finishing her sentence for her. Dish towel in hand, I appear in the doorway. I lean against the marred threshold, cracked mortar and displaced nails. "Never forget who you're talking to. I was once the child of a master gardener."

"Does it make you sad—thinking about them?"

"Not as sad as when I knew they were thinking about me."

"But it's all right," she offers—"to be sad when you think of them *not* thinking of you. It's only human to want the things we can't have."

"Does it say there what the aster means?"

Angie smoothes a fine crease, and now the paper crackles under her hand. "Only that it's Latin for *star* . . . oh, and in one myth, asters were created from Virgo's tears, when she looked down from Heaven and wept. That's a bit melodramatic, I think."

"Asters," I tell her, "have long been considered the flowers of afterthought." The kettle now, beginning to wail.

"Why?"

"In France during the War, families laid asters on the graves of fallen soldiers. They represented—*you'll love this*—the wish that things had turned out differently."

I carry a small, wooden tray into the living room and place it on the coffee table. This pleases me inexplicably—the act of serving coffee on a coffee table. A smug, tidy feeling accompanies my task, as if this correspondence of object and function—this correlation of names—has realigned our universe, imposed order where chaos once had been.

The stillness, however, cannot last long. Passing over the Obituaries en route to the Op-Ed page, a name rises up, accompanied by a black-and-white photograph and a bolded phrase. "What is it?" Angie asks. I cannot explain, so she takes the paper from me and reads aloud: "Linda A. Wade, 58, died yesterday from complications with breast cancer. She is survived by her mother June, her brother Bill, and her sister-in-law, Linda. Ms. Wade will be buried in the family plot at Washington Memorial Cemetery, now Bonney-Watson. Private services to be held. In lieu of flowers, please make a donation to the National Audubon Society, of which Ms. Wade was a devoted member."

Too startled for tears, I can only tremble: "But she had gone into remission. She had told me—she said it herself—there was nothing to worry about."

"What can I do? Tell me what I can do."

"I have to call my father. I have to call him."

"Julie—wait."

"For what? What am I waiting for? I've already waited too long!"

"He doesn't know you. He won't understand."

"Then, I have to make him understand. I met him by the river. It was Christmastime. Aunt Linda was still alive then. I promised to give him a story."

Now the fragrance of the lilacs assaults my senses, fills me with an unexpected rage. Now the rain, strumming the windows, strikes me as calculating, cruel.

Angie follows me into the kitchen, wrests the phone from my hand. "Listen to me. Just listen. Before you do anything rash, you need to remember that they didn't forget you. There is no malice in this. They never had the choice to forget you."

"But I didn't forget *them*! No matter what happens, I'll always know that they're my family. Their grief is still my grief; their loss is still my loss." I am crying now, tears that have been pending for years.

"Yes. But that is *your* cross to bear, not theirs. And if you call them now, or try to interfere, you're only going to scare them or confuse them. They can't see you for who you really are."

"But I thought—at the back of my mind, you know—that I could meet them, not as their daughter, just as another person in the world, and that we could grow to care for each other, that we would become *like family* . . . but without all the guilt, without all the baggage."

"So it was your intention all along to go back? You never meant to make a fresh start?"

"No—I mean—maybe. I don't know. I thought if I wasn't family, they'd have less invested in me—no name to live up to, no legacy to carry on. I thought, if I couldn't make things *right*, at least maybe I could make them *different*."

Angie is standing at the counter, her hand on my shoulder, her voice in my ear: "But don't you see? You left because they wanted to change you. Now you're here because you want to change them. That doesn't seem different to me, Love. That seems exactly the same."

Parable Which Begins with a Cemetery and Ends with an
   Airplane

Washington Memorial remains, despite its altered name, along International Boulevard near Sea-Tac Airport. I have come here not unlike George Bailey, in his grimmest hour, wandering among the gravestones of this potter's field. Angie waits in the cab with our bags: some we will check and some we will carry on. Cut from our own garden, I hold a harvest of late-summer asters in my hands.

The grave is there, just as I imagined it: small and spare, carved without flourish. In the corner, a familiar stencil: bright dove bearing an olive branch; God's promise that he will never again destroy the earth with water.

"But what about all the other ways we could be destroyed?" I had demanded upon first hearing the Bible story.

"If you have enough faith," my father replied, "you won't have to think so hard."

Because I don't know what to do or say—because there is a way that sorrow always comes too late, even as grief is consistently foreshadowed—I stand a long time in silence, thinking of my family, and my thoughts mingle with the most recent poem I have read. When my own words fail me, I think of what a poet has said:

Nothing lasts.
There is a graveyard where everything I am talking about is,
now.

I stood there once, on the green grass, scattering flowers.
— Mary Oliver, "Flare"

So here I stand, on the green grass, scattering the long-stemmed, blue-faced flowers of afterthought. Everything is an afterthought now.

But unlike the poet, whose work I have long admired, I cannot make this promise:

I mention them now,
I will not mention them again.

"I will mention you," I tell my Aunt Linda. "I will mention them, too."

It is not lack of love
nor lack of sorrow.
But the iron thing they carried, I will not carry.

"I will make a space for you—all of you—in this story that is also my life." Speaking to the birds now, the trees: "This story that is never only my life."

Now for the poet's last dictum: *Scatter your flowers over the graves, and walk away.*

I will do it, because I must. Because there is the whole business of my beautiful life to get back to. I will walk away, the flowers under my feet, but often I will stop and look back.

In this nowhere-time, this every-place, Angie and I stand at the gate, somewhat encumbered, our fingers furtively laced. We have passed the security checkpoint; we have ridden on the crowded tram. I am no more or less orphaned than the last time we left, but my birth certificate returns to my bag.

Epilogue

Mr. Bill Wade, Industrial Engineer
Boeing Company, Plant 2
Duamish River Parkway

Enclosed please find the story I promised to share.

—JMW

Parable in Which Immanuel Kant Meets George Bailey at a Carnival

Frank Capra would not direct this piece, which he felt did not support the "triumph of the individual spirit" over the collective will. Rather, the two men encountered each other without fanfare or supervision on a crisp autumn night, somewhere in Prussia or upstate New York. Location is not so important. And as the Ferris wheel offered a pleasant alternative to walking around in circles, both men approached it apace and were seated together in a single chair.

"You know," Kant remarked, as they were moving steadily through the night sky, "I feel I must tell you that your wish to end your life is contrary to the notion of perfect duty."

"Perhaps," Bailey considered, "but there seems no other way to move in the world without causing harm. Wouldn't it be better to choose this single and final harm than to continue along a course of cumulative failure?"

"No, sir, I do not believe it would."

"All right then, forget about death," Bailey instructed with a sweep of his hand. "What about the possibility of non-being, of never having even been born?"

"I was not aware there was such a possibility," replied Kant,

"for if there were, how would we, the beings in question, see fit to unslip such a treacherous knot?"

"But if we were," Bailey urged. "If we were."

They had come to a stop, as often happens, their star positioned at the outermost point of the constellation. "I find your question to be at odds with the fundamental laws of moral duty," Kant returned after some moments of silent contemplation. "I would classify it as 'intent to break promise,' which is different," he quickly added, "from breaking promise without intent."

"How so?" the Everyman asked the Philosopher.

"Well, it's quite simple, Mr. Bailey. Existence obligates you to try. That is the covenant, whether chosen or not. If you have tried and failed, so be it, but the failure to try is far more sinister. In fact, 'the universality of a law which says that anyone believing himself to be in difficulty could promise whatever he pleases with the intention of not keeping it would make promising itself and the end to be attained thereby quite impossible.'"

"But I've promised nothing," Bailey protested. "I've only asked to be erased, stricken, as it were, from the cosmic record."

"You've promised something by drawing breath," Kant insisted. "You've promised something by having the foresight and desire to formulate a wish. If everyone were to wish as you did, and all such wishes to be granted, the wish would reveal itself a universal maxim of destruction. No good could come from it."

George Bailey did not have a rebuttal. Immanuel Kant did not expect him to. Instead, they sat quietly rocking against that pin-drop night, two still points in a turning world.

Oh but you have to learn to let her go you said
out into the open field through the waiting the waving grasses
way out to the edge of that drastic field of distinctions
each new possibility molting off the back of the one motion,
    creation,
until there are so many truths each one its own color
it's a flower the picking of which would open the world
the mouth over the unsaid whispering loves me not loves me

—Jorie Graham,
from "Self-Portrait as Demeter and Persephone"

Personal Acknowledgments

This book is an elegy for many I have loved and lost. It is for my parents, Linda and Bill; my grandmother June (1911–2008); my Aunt Linda (1945–2004); also, for my grandfather John (1911–1971) and my great aunt Ruth (1897–1993). Finally: for Bob Parker (1925–2010) and Robyn Dawes (1936–2010), two incomparable minds I was lucky to know and learn from.

Many thanks to all my friends, teachers, and mentors over these first thirty-two years. Each of you has left a welcome imprint on my life: Fatin Abdul-Sabur, Annette Allen, Connie Angermeier, Bruce Beasley, Linda Breuer, April Davis, Ben Dobyns, Carolyn DuPen, Becky Farrell, Lucy Fischer, Kathryn Flannery, Cate Fosl, Paul Griner, Dustin Hall, Jason Hanson, Katie Hogan, Mandy Holbrook, Sister Janice Holkup, Holly Holland, Beth Kraig, Kara Larson, Patsy Maloney, Sally McLaughlin, Joy Meyers, Brenda Miller, John Miller, Christine Moon, Charles Mudede, Anna Murray, Vanessa Ortblad, Suzanne Paola, Sister Rosemary Perisich, Donna Qualley, Kerry Reynolds, Star Rush, Maggie Santolla, Sarah Scholl, David Seal, Bill Smith, Barbara Temple-Thurston, Jen Thonney, Steve Vanderstaay, and Gabe Yu.

Special thanks to Sarah Gorham, Caroline Casey, Kirby Gann, and all the Sarabandistas—for believing in this work and shepherding it to print.

My deepest gratitude and enduring affection extend always to Dana Anderson, Tom Campbell, Rev Culver, James Allen Hall, Monica Krupinski, James Leary, Jess Leary, Keely Lewis, Sara Northerner, Lisa Parker, Amy Patterson, Elijah Pritchett, Anna Rhodes, Carol Stewart, the Striegel family—Kim, Matt, Evie, and Nolan, aka "Super Baby Hondo"—Helena Studer, Amy Tudor, and Steve Watkins. (Dear Lunas and Swole-Mates, you know who you are!)

Most of all, for Angie Griffin, my partner through three degrees, four states, and nine years: "there isn't a particle of you that I don't know, remember, and want."

Literary Acknowledgments

"Keepsake" appears in the Spring 2009 issue of *Redivider*.

"Triptych of My Grandmother . . ." appears in the Fall 2010 issue of *South Loop Review Online*.

"Three Keys" appears in the Summer 2008 issue of *Under the Sun*.

"Triptych of My Mother . . ." appears in the Summer/Fall 2009 issue of *So to Speak: A Feminist Journal of Language and Art*.

"Skin" received the 2010 *Arts & Letters* Nonfiction Prize. It appears in the Spring 2011 issue of *Arts & Letters: A Journal of Contemporary Culture*.

"Four Eyes in a Dark Room" received second place for the Mary C. Mohr Nonfiction Prize. It appears in the Summer 2009 issue of *Southern Indiana Review*.

"Triptych of My Aunt Linda . . ." appears in the Spring 2009 issue of *The MacGuffin*.

"Meditation 29" appears in the Winter 2011 issue of *New Delta Review*.

"Traveling" appears in the Winter 2007 issue of *Sonora Review*.

"Triptych of My Father . . ." appears in the Summer/Fall 2009 issue of *So to Speak: A Feminist Journal of Language and Art*.

"The Flower of Afterthought" appears in the Summer 2008 issue of *Fourteen Hills: The San Francisco State University Review*.